The Postmortem Condition

A philosophical inventory by

David E. Perugini

This book is dedicated to Dr. Michael Sugrue and Dr. Darren Staloff, two professors without whom my education would never have progressed far enough to bring these ideas to fruition, though neither has ever met me in person.

The Penitent Wisdom

I

The sick man needs a physician; the sick mankind needs a metaphysician. I find myself in a world of many contradictions and untreated symptoms. For starters, knowledge is more abundant than at any point in recorded history, yet most restrict themselves to a small section of it, preferring to extrapolate their Grand Unifying Truth from the limited sample that satisfies them rather than to seek the largest possible scope of resolution. Pretense is valued over substance. This is true of both the academic and the commoner. In a similar vein, the sheer abundance of knowledge, codified in written language, engenders a seemingly-exponential problem for anyone with the ambition to undertake a broad understanding of history and/or the human condition. The *punctuated equilibrium* of academic progress is no longer sufficient. What once served as a vehicle of intellectual freedom, both from the State and Nature, has stagnated to the point of reinforcing the tyranny of both.

I would need ten Kantian lifetimes to accomplish one tenth of a Kant! Fortunately for me, the stock price of wisdom has plummeted dreadfully since his time. The post-world is intellectually-bankrupt, and I have come to buy the controlling share. Adjusting for inflation, surely this cannot be a foolhardy investment! The apparatchiks will no doubt sneer and protest. I care not. I will serve as either parody or prophet, God as my judge. *And if these words all be in vain, I gladly piss upon the flames!*

Religion became science and science became religion, in a sense. We thought we could think our way out of the jar, and merely flipped our minds upside-down. We stand agape at the sheer material scale of the universe on the one hand, which we are made rationally aware of via modern cosmology, and yet we persist culturally in a twofold delusion on the other: 1) that the universe was unknown or unknowable before modern materialism, and 2) that advances in natural science somehow invalidate (the concept of) mystical wisdom or experiences rather than elucidate, compliment, or vindicate them. The modern secular intellectual is forced to appeal to blind chance proportional to their scientistic sentimentality. You may argue, if you wish, that the probability of what has already occurred is 1, but that is a word game pretending to be metaphysics, ultimately sophistry, and avoids the valid human intuition that the universe *ought* to have an explanation, an intelligible order, rather than merely a set of immutable rules immaterial to our subjective experience – ultimately a negation of subjectivity altogether.

This brings us to perhaps the most damning or visible contradiction: the gap between public perception of the state of scientific and technological advancement versus the objective reality of the progression of physics, which is the hardest of the sciences and the discipline ultimately responsible for what is called the "cutting edge". We have fallen under the spell of media; fiction does not reward partial credit to reality, no matter how imaginative. You must show your work. Force equals mass times acceleration, not ambition. The short version: Nietzsche warned us.

The state religion of scientism, appropriate to a technocracy, has exhausted the fumes it generated by burning monotheism for fuel (and the particulates in the atmosphere have become problematic). Meanwhile, the average prole still goes to work as if the Space Age is actually just around the corner; I have now lived long enough to observe it hiding just around the corner for several decades, like a thief, with no (profitable) logistical advances. The average prole either does not know this or does not care because, sadly, propaganda and profiteering have replaced education. The Westerner has grown tired of questioning. Questioning without Truth is a hamster wheel, amusing at best.

Alas, I am not so well-read. Doubtful I am first to observe: *Science is dead.* But fear not! As science is a product of God, it may rise again. Nietzsche, as opposed to Your Humble Noisemaker, was extremely well-read, but when he sang the requiem for the Almighty, he had forgotten what came to pass the time when man killed God the last.

I have no presumption of moral judgment of the past, but perhaps the use of the fission bomb was a kind of choice, a kind of spell: a powerful sacrilege. From *some* point on, if not that particular one, science became a corpse: reanimated into undying service by the State-Industrial Complex, the most fearsome of all necromancers. We could have powered the world; instead we chose power for its own sake. We could have had enlightenment; we chose immolation. And we think we can have it both ways.

In fact, it probably occurred long before that; all real phenomena emerge gradually in any case, all the way down to the quanta. What is relevant, to my mind, is that Christ lay in the tomb for three days, and Lazarus, four. A zeitgeist of revival is prevailing over the looming despair of dying empires. And when *He is risen* once more, soon after will follow the utopian age of which with childlike reverie we dream.

"Science is real!" they credulously declare, as if protesting the obsolescence of last year's pagan patron. Do they read academic journals or engage in methodological experimentation? Have they any notion of the scope of specialization into which modern science has diffused, or the economic value of what to which our public wealth has been sacrificed? Advances in physics were once the prime mover of our *great* industrial economy. The plebeian cry of "Where are the flying cars?" deserves an answer, however plebeian its formulation. But there is no answer – only *great* experimental machines (and the technocrats that pull the financial levers) whose size and cost is proportional to their cosmic hilarity. Of course, the occasional individual makes it their business to self-educate, or perhaps has a natural inclination to engage in experimentation outside the auspice of an institution, but as is ever the case, individuals remain occasional and beleaguered. (And of course, there is little left to discover on one's coffee table (or so you hope)).

To those only partially-awake, to borrow what is now a tired cliché, such slogans evoke a feeling that used to refer to Something, but now occupies their memory as a hanging pointer, to borrow from the programming world. The advent of computer science is pregnant with lessons on the human condition, most of which entirely hidden from the view of those, as in any time, are content to live as if the current age is the final one: this too being a perversion of eschatology. The End Times necessitate *Something* subsequent.

To say one last thing of the particle accelerator: I can imagine many an angel finding laughter, as we humans occasionally do, upon observing the *height* of human technological progress: wherein the clever cavemen smash bits of space together, to glimpse what cosmic confections come forth. Never has so little material knowledge been extracted at so great a material cost, never so extreme an asymptote graphed: *if only we could build a ring the size of the galaxy, then we could go all the way back!* We learned far more smashing bugs with rocks – *and that cost all of about zero kilowatts!*

The more I look at culture, the more I realize that works which are not divinely-inspired (whether in claim or actuality, for the power of God cannot be stolen or imitated), amounts to little more than randomly or procedurally-generated sensory stimuli: shaking keys in the face of an infant, *pretty lights* on the cave wall. That which does not refer, at some point in the *genealogy* of its ideation, to God, invariably refers to nothing. The aestheticism reflects the macrocosmic perception. *It's all a great big random nothing; draw Platonic solids on the canvas; it's so valued that only aristocrats can afford to buy it!* At any rate, thieves need launder their ill-gotten gains.

The artist and the intellectual were both granted their vain wish for social elevation. They were raised up to such height that they could no longer hear the Signal they relied upon to perceive things *as they are* (Inverse Square Law!). They coveted thrones and ironically failed to calculate the weight of crowns, the effect of political machination upon peripheral vision, of wealth upon salvation. They gave up trying to calculate salvation long ago- justifiably so! But I must state an eternal banality: if they had not done so, I would not be here to say so. That is, history is not a series of tangential misadventures; it is a singular adventure, a singular (mystery) History. *I am to stand on the shoulders of giants, and thou canst stopeth me not; for in thy race to God replace, thou hath summoned a dreadnaught.*

Pray to your strange god of Reason that the bonds of your structures may absorb dauntless this free radical what furious energy possess, however lowly it may read upon material measurement. Feel free (and rational) to recalibrate your instruments. I will use what tools I have been given. I will demolish the brick with a toothpick wearing clown white if I must – *and when the toothpick doth inevitably fail, I shall press into service my fingernail!*

Why do the thinkers among the species labor (such as it is) under the delusion that they must *liberate*? I can suppose many answers; they are all insipid (and doubtless unoriginal!).

Technology advanced in my lifetime such that I could witness a digital video recording of a chimpanzee wielding an automatic rifle. This life has been a museum of images so cosmically-laughable that one resolves each, in soul-crushing succession, sufficient to be the last thing one might as well ever witness. No combination of English letters could say more about this sobbing circus clown of a century than that chimp feeling the dopamine rush of a mag dump while numerous *greater* apes look on with shock and awe.

Fiction used to be stranger than truth. Oh how they laughed and played! Fiction cowers in fear of truth these days. For fiction, it was all fun and games while truth in the back room was shooting dope in' its veins. Fiction keeps up the one dance it knows, bowing a dour dirge as the greatest (most unsinkable) ship in history drinks the briny abyss.

I will not even speak of the "B&C". You hear me? I will conjure the very spirit of Jeremiah to scream at thee if I hear it mentioned once more. Public education has infected discourse with such insufferable dilettantery that even millennia-old lessons remain opaque irony. Can we learn and move on already? Can we laugh at the past for a change instead of it laughing at us, and us (ironically) at ourselves?

The machine man laughs all the way to hell (only a simulation).

II

The universe is a hologram – not to be confused with a shadow of Heaven, no sir! – but indeed to be confused with a science-fictional account of a "hologram". The proles preferred the fiction, less math. Pearls before swine, alas!

The ennui of *no more adventures*: The body is for overcoming space, the mind for overcoming time, and that is only four dimensions out of the ten that the grand magi have sketched out. Despair not! We may need not the sky to open after all! If we can only wake the sleepy hearts of the materialist miners, even if only to a paltry science-fiction, those of us few and stubborn embers may kindle the rest. And for those more-exasperated souls for want of less grandiose a trade: our so-called conquest of the first four dimensions still leaves much to be desired. *To your tents!*

You can take George's Geist and shove it up Freddy's Antichrist. *I mean no offense! Don't mind me! I'm all wound-up, you see: ever since they strapped me and fastened open my glazzies.*

How can I be expected to act naturally?

Let the Ivory Tower of Babel fall. Let them reap what they have sown. Let them choke upon *this* irony: it is but the *great* godless Übermensch that wants for an ark. To build their own, they have neither wood nor worker – not for lack of supply but for lack of vision! There simply is not enough material upon the Earth to build it. Their designs are, shall we say, somewhat uninspired. I will endeavor not to be too cruel, for want of not of speaking ill of the terminally-ill.

One, two, three, four, Friedrich declared a time war. Upon his head, inscribeth he "Goliath", and thrust his banner in' the ground in triumph. Alas, his mental stature vast, if only the giant had reach.

You must know that I respect this man as much as he respected Socrates – and this I state with no irony! He played his part with singular virtuosity, *God's beloved canary.* Your Humble Noisemaker can only hope to be of such utility, and never of such talent.

Here stands this *liberated* prole, to so-presumptuously audit the Empire of Dirt: whose major exports are waste heat and mold, who for a single meal its birthright sold; whose guilt-ridden effetes – excuse me, *elites* – cannot buy the Stairway with gold. –

Oh don't get me wrong, don't misunderstand! I'm happy to hear out your alternative plan. But if thee turn out to be more-over-than-Overman, pack it in, learn a trade, I rightly demand, thou Inebriated Icarian, Preconceived Principali-dan, would-be Purple Praetorian. Man Made Dirigible in a hydrogen gale. Tasteless, baseless, hero-accountant: find thy bottom line in the red. *There is but one thing one can purchase with debt.*

I must extend the sportsman's hand: to my friend, Freddy, to be my strawman. For only a mind as sensitive as his would dare have sympathy for the devil.

After all, who could cast a stone at Pilate, who watched a people murder their God? He was merely a tool. He provided nothing more than choice. Here lies your metaphysique: where choice was buried alive.

III

Art cannot liberate the *masses* any more than a prophet can liberate livestock. It may shine like the sun and they will see only straw. Art must impinge upon the mind via the senses. What one needs is a *firmware update.* At least two points are needed to draw a line, and three for a shape. So God can no longer be found in the state; didst thou look anywhere else? For my part, I can say that God has been blaring at all the world through the trumpet of art – music, but the call seems only heard by us brow-beaten mutts.

Perhaps it is for the best. After all, is it the *sheep* that need liberation? Is it the dutiful worker that needs *our* help? Ha! They seem quite capable of looking after themselves – even unto suffering and death! A worker does not want to be *liberated.* You know what a worker wants? A safe place to live, food in their fridge, and the best possible tools to do their job. If you can give people that, they'll come damned close to calling you God, and if you know what is best for all, you will kindly remind them – That you are not.

You think Jesus never laughed because it was not recorded in the Gospels? Tell me, why would one record the commonplace alongside the anything-but? If I know Him, and I believe that I do, quite the giggle He derives from all you. We laugh to allay the pain, do we not?

"Man plans and God laughs", but it took man's suffering to make God cry. And it took God crying to make man *know* his suffering. Ever so often, there is a breakthrough, and you might say that the Lord was on a roll in those days.

Our metaphysics have not changed. This is fitting since metaphysics are not an aspect of existence that we *can* change. But we persist as if some grand transition occurred that separates our modern psyche from its state, say, a couple thousand, or even a few hundred years ago. There is some truth in this, as in all misapprehensions, but we have taken for granted the things with which we are born. The materialist world only recently shrugged off the misadventure of tabula rasa, and not yet even to the extent that all materialists have abandoned their utopian dreams that rely utterly on such a notion. The average citizen with a public education is of course more factually knowledgeable about the world than their socioeconomic equivalent in past eras, but the *meta* of the human condition is not something one can arbitrarily reconfigure inter-generationally, if at all. The most straightforward consequence of this is that when people think about religion and God, both theist and atheist, there is a stubborn lack of clarity between the metaphysical concept and human social conventions or institutions. The materialist, the apostate, and the parishioner all default to equivocation between *God* and *Church*. It is a metaphysical or linguistic trap that emerges when one is too zealous with the chainsaw of rationalism and severs that artery feeding the part of your brain that allows for metaphysics in the first place: as a part of the world (or more correctly: the world as a part of it) and not merely an abstract symbol for academic discussion. This chainsaw, however, cannot destroy the humanitarian need for metaphysical belief. In a way: today's scientistic citizen is yesterday's *Good Catholic*. They appeal to an earthly authority while their eyes are to the stars. Their faith, such as it is, ultimately is in the state.

And this brings us to the scientistic contradiction of treating Methodological Naturalism as though it were some *new and improved!* metaphysics: capable-with-ease of filling the God-shaped hole. This is difficult to describe, but easy to perceive – my earlier example of "Science is real!" could not have been foreign. It is common to hear people speak of Science, not in a clinical or academic tone, but by stating pedestrian affirmations of belief or astonishment. Machine man *believes* in Science: giver of all knowledge and quality of life. No need for prayers, or faith, or good works, or (God forbid) self-denial; the only commandment is to pay your taxes!

Another consequence of this is our tendency to play out the same collectivistic social patterns that for which the secular world loves to criticize religion: our tribalism, dogmatism, and even schism. If one can hold one's laughter at the irony long enough to briefly research the history of organized atheism, one would witness such a pattern as would-be apostles (one wonders if with any self-awareness) attempt to build their ill-conceived church before your very eyes. Whatever this pattern is at its core, it would seem that human nature is either greatly attracted to it or greatly fettered by it: a self-fulfilling prophecy of a bleary-eyed race.

The bigger picture here, as I began before, is that far less has changed about our psyche over the past 2,000 years than we like to think, apart from one very important thing: the emergence of the individual. Do not foolishly put the cart before the horse and blame philosophy. *We sensitive boys are all merely canaries in our own way.* Oh I can shake my fist at Marx, let me assure you! But I cannot help but see a small piece of myself inside that arrogant bastard too. *Lord, help me to love my enemies. I refuse, however, to wash their feet. Amen.*

Theology is possibly blasphemous and certainly futile. But don't let that stop you!

It would be highly unoriginal to point out the philosophical link between Marxism (or any Utopian socialist ideology) and Christianity, yet the average prole does not make this association. The pile of evidence of the (on-going, one might say *progressive*) failure of public education continues to mount, this being one small piece of a great many. The typical prole is not *liberated*. They are well-fed and entertained (so help me!), their life expectancy has been increased and infant mortality reduced, etc., but their consciousness (or indeed their conscience, if you prefer) has stagnated.

Those of us with a vague understanding of God, have we not warned you? It is the way of man to take things for granted, even his own consciousness. It is one thing to think of oneself as an animal in the abstract, a kind of exercise in humility, but machine man takes it too far, and never ceases to invent excuses for his actions; the uptime of his self-awareness wanes. He laughs ironically at himself as the paint peels around him.

We live in a ruin. You only disagree because you are not, as it turns out, quite so forward-thinking.

Man *is* liberated through art in a sense: we may channel the emotional tension that builds up from navigating a world of hypocritical self-interest – like a car eking through a mountain tunnel that is too small not to scrape against the sides. *We didn't ask for this, etc.*

But at a certain point (for God's sake), something has to correlate! I mean being human, particularly in the process of self-improvement, entails a certain occasional or quiescent hypocrisy, but as the gulf between reality and the fiction to which we escape expands, so too does our necessary hypocrisy, our heteronomy, perhaps our *alienation*, and I would argue as well our mental aberration. *BLAH, BLAH, BLAH – UNAHPPY PEOPLE, POVERTY, MISERY, POWER POLITICS, ET CETERA.* I'm sorry; I was starting to bore even myself.

I suppose it is the nature of stagnation – cultural, technological, or otherwise – that the very awareness of it is unpopular.

Over a sufficient time scale, all lies are unsustainable.

IV

"Ontology capitulates phylogeny": I had something like this happen to me over the course of my life with philosophy, as if I were retracing the contemplative path of the archetypal Western Man. I very much had a Nietzsche phase, what seems like a lifetime ago. I suppose now I am in my Kierkegaard phase. Hard to imagine what comes after that! Armageddon, I suppose; that makes me quite useless as a philosopher as well, as each of us is apparently meant to elaborate some New Grand Unifying Truth (NewGUT), declare ourselves The End, and murder all those that came before us, like peripatetic Sith. Fine; you (man) want to write your own story. But it is always the same story. Big monkey make bigger gun. Monkey god.

I have nothing (yet) worthwhile to say about 20th century philosophy. The last 120 years have been a gallery of examples of harsh and disgusting variety. ("Examples of what?" Pick your poison.) Our philosophy was no bright light either (except for maybe Bergson; Wittgenstein was a genius, but logical positivism was the Manhattan Project of philosophy). Thinking became an industry like mining; they plumbed so deep that soon they couldn't rightly discern their anus from the hole in the ground that they had dug! *They murdered Truth; there was no one to tell them which was which.* Theirs became the philosophy of infantile regression and nihilism, with a dose of Satanic pride. I'm standing here with a literal axe to grind like John the Baptist.

And we are still in the 20th century, and still in the Year of our Lord. You can think about time in terms of the cyclical motions of the heavenly bodies if you want, or the soulless nomenclature of the "Common Era", but it seems somewhat primitive to me, not to mention extremely boring. To each his own![1]

---

[1] Made you look!

Call me a simpleton, but I do think philosophy should be a kind of trade, like plumbing or fishing, rather than a *higher* academic pursuit (maybe nothing should be a *higher* academic pursuit). In practice, you do not need an ivory tower from which orthodoxy is trickled down upon the flock, or even a mountain of text that gains in elevation with every passing age. It was fine when it was just a bunch of Greek stoners from the suburbs. In practice, what is needed, for every thousand-or-so people, is a *stranger* among them: someone to walk a *mysterious* path, to the annoyance of everyone else: not-quite-hunting and not-quite-gathering. This *doctor of life* dispenses the medicine of wisdom and cultural enrichment to their people as needed, and both the doctor and the patient exist as part of an organic whole. There would be no need for one to travel far and wide or administer to many, for such persons are not *so* rare, and the medicine of one tribe might not be fit for another – unless of course there occurs some kind of *breakthrough... Wait, no! Is that not how we got into this mess?*

An historian is just a ditch-digger that tries to work smarter instead of harder.

Oppenheimer helps crucify the nucleus and then waxes poetic from Eastern scriptures. At least the schmuck who touched the Ark had a quick death. Never did get my rocket boots.

Of course *we* feel guilty for everything. Our ideas have more destructive power than our physical weapons. Splitting the atom, after all, only destroyed two cities. And both of those cities are remarkably thriving less than a century later. Meanwhile, the mass grave of (recent) history bears earthen, often oblivious host to a fossil record of psychic victims: a desolated temporal battlefield where people enlisted to become things.

No one feels empathy for a robot until the robot starts asking *religious* questions. Up until that point, you can stick its head in a hydraulic press.

This is not to say that human empathy is any great marvel: humans have become small; I have seen them project onto a single-celled organism, a microscopic video. It died, one presumes, from a pH-imbalance with its environment or one of the thousand other reasons that microbes expire every biological moment. One might have thought that they had witnessed a whole person fall into a volcano. This object/subject crisis is emerging, has emerged everywhere in the Western conscience. We are losing the sense of where we end and the world begins.

Passionless pursuit of power or passionate projection of pathos: take your pick, Superman. As the young whippersnappers would say: *I cringe my last meme at thee!*

The worst thing about this secular world is that it seems to believe that it is not a secular world. It hides behind the comfortable denial often provided by statistical analysis. It does not embrace its direction. It has none. It behaves like a pagan: proud when fortunate, pathetic when unfortunate, never aware of its own precariousness, and never evolving in its substance. The side-effect of secular eternity is hostility to change, ironically enough. Material science has backslid in the mind of the prole: back to the pagan nature spirits of old. Leave it to the high priests to understand and impart their ways. And they understand them perfectly, do not blaspheme! We shall make you sit in the corner with a hat made of aluminum foil, and we shall laugh at you! Machines by their very design go in circles.

The magi found, one might say *figured*, the soul to be a perfect cube. In their genius they deduced: a square-shaped hole we need only produce and the soul would fit inside safe and sound. No God needed it turns out! The Sword of Occam proved quite sharp indeed! – Alas, irony of ironies! Of all the heroes to face all the tragedies: the physicists failed to account for spin.

If I am crude or cantankerous, it is because if Armageddon does not come in this lifetime, we will be spending it with a spiked stick picking up the wretched refuse of your steaming shore. And then, when we have collected all your depleted uranium and recycled plastic, if we have children, we will need to raise them in a milieu very foreign from the one you knew, and fashion for them from your garbage humble wreaths of wisdom. They will have to earn the grace of God again, and spend a twilight stacking bricks and mortar. We will praise them not for being special but for being soldiers.

Who am I talking to...? No one. Myself. Dead people. Satan.

Philosophy forms a celebrated part of our culture and the backbone of our civilization, and yet if you act like Socrates in any social/group setting, honestly questioning the meaning and logic of another person's thoughts, they want to kill you as much as the sophists wanted to kill the Good Inquirer. And one wonders if maybe they were right, not about sophistry but about getting rid of the guy *harshing the vibe*: who could famously hold his liquor like a human keg, and denied the lusts of other men during what was, even up to now, truly the *gayest* time. They could probably feel him entering the room before they even turned around – the Truth, the ugly, irritating, incessant, indefatigable Truth: looming like a nimbus come to rain down self-awareness 'pon their blissful parade of sin. *Oh Christ, not this asshole again.*

V

You believe it is the year 2023; in fact, it is closer to the year 123. This is the world as it appears today:

Fear & Trembling in La Vega: We were somewhere between Violins and Orgies, near the edge of the desert, when the drugs began to take hold. My God, was that top-down convertible screaming through Bat Country a horrifyingly prescient metaphor. I was that naive idiot kid, who had as fate would have it, hitched a ride backseat the American Dream: where there was "no communication". His simple mind becomes less-so by minute, and reels in curious disgust, bearing witness powerless, accessory to the boomer journalist and his doctor/lawyer/accomplice, as they prescribe to one another bad narcotics and worse advice, on a quixotic quest to revel in obscene excess. At least they admired the shape of my skull.

The 20ᵗʰ century had few philosophers of any lasting value. Hunter S. Thomson was one of them. The modern philosopher cannot be a monk or pretentious academic; the Geist (if you are into that sort of thing) has been developing within popular culture, and wallowing in the mire of our bloated bride Babylon. The same revelations that were always there in nature, when one strips off the baggage of the world and walks the ascetic path, are still there, as a starting point, but Spirit simply has more tools to express itself in the sea of symbols modern English has become, not to mention digital media with which to reach the minds of many. This comes back to my friend, HST, for to even navigate – let alone fish upon – this sea of symbols, one must be able to adequately *apply tension* to one's being (becoming). Surely he was no moral exemplar, like a true boomer, he took it too far. But I would say of his death, the 21ˢᵗ century: will find nothing more alike to Socrates' Apology.

He described his craft, in often self-deprecating terms, as "gonzo journalism". I will not attempt to define it here. I am not even completely sure what it is. But I knew once I beheld it that what was needed was a kind of *gonzo philosophy*: for us postmodern pod people to come to grips with the *Circus, Circus* that is our lives; to hurl oneself into the middle of all chaos, to become chaos – saturated with it until it can no longer harm us like the Spice Mélange – as "He was counted amongst wrongdoers", to absorb and refract all sin and falsehood like a crystal prism, and decry in the most divine and baffling terms the true nature of the corruption extant, like the prophets and shamans of Old.

You must *apply tension to being*, to borrow the phraseology of Terence McKenna (oh I'll get to him, don't you worry!), to get beyond the great tides of symbols along in which we all get swept. This is not a new idea by any means. In fact, it is the oldest idea! Merely our orientation toward this thing is what must change, if we want to unlock the next stage. This is the Key, if you will, the Boss Key!

It is all about separating Signal from Noise, and one does that in a particular way: by increasing resolution. Your consciousness is naturally evolved to seek physical truths, not metaphysical ones; to process sensory data, not lead you like a sleeping sheep right to the Kingdom of Heaven. The concept of 'sobriety' can be misleading. It implies a center that does not truly exist, or at best, does so only as homeostasis, which varies from individual to individual both in terms of objective measurement and subjective experience, and varies still further over a lifetime. You *triangulate* truth by experiencing the psycho-motive tension between disparate states of awareness. At all times and places, the most accessible methods of achieving such altered states have been fasting and meditation. These practices have never been arbitrary, irrespective of specific religion, their value, as with all things, is in the ends they achieve. There is a blunt simplicity to fasting and meditation. In a way, they are highly irrational activities, and yet we now have compelling evidence of their physical value even besides spiritual traditions. I suspect our ancient war with nature may have been our incidental teacher of these techniques through times of forced starvation and reflection. Even unintentional alterations in diet can induce such states. In fact, my very thesis here is that the mind is not a finite state machine at all, but something more *infinite.* I suspect some of us simply need stronger medicine than we did in the time before Christ. Whether this is a matter of density of cultural novelty, neurology, or perhaps a matter of having fallen even further, I cannot say, but the nonzero value of the experience of altered states I can deny neither in myself nor in others within our cultural record. As with many things, it is the individuation of both physiological and psychological response that makes this a difficult subject. If an experience causes one person to change their while life for the better, while causing another to lose their mind and never recover, it is hard to say for certain if that thing is good or bad for a person. It seems more fitting to say only that it is a choice for a person. Statistics are often a crutch for our discourse. Statistics can tell you nothing about what it is like to be a human.

Materialism is a sharpened inclined plane that must be fashioned into machetes and lawnmower blades instead of swords and systems that cut us down to size. The *next* man, if you will, the *synthesized* man, the *psilocyborg* keeps what is useful and is not weighed down by temporal trifles or collectivistic contrivances. There is nothing more useful than God, and God abides neither falsehood nor waste. Think it over, if you please. I leave each mensch to, in his own way, walk his path with no regard what I say. *But without God, the only Borg is the Collective. If only Karl and Fred could have lived to dread it.*

Let us be candid, if only for a moment: the paradigm of making humans subservient to machines, instead of the other way around, is, in both hindsight *and* foresight, since art *is* after all the modern medium of prophecy (and the ancient medium warned us as well!), so unrepentantly-stupid and degenerate in every sense, that were it not for the Sixth Commandment, I could rationally recommend no more-justified a course of action than to exterminate with prejudice both dispassionate and extreme any Western person who may be called leader or politician. I would say let them abdicate (physically, as they long ago did so ethically) all power and treasure and walk away: with that they can purchase back their life-debt to the body-poli-whereupon-they-tick.

This, of course, is nothing more than a proletarian revolution in so many words. It is the same choice as always: mass of the living God or mass graves, Sinai or Stalin. You think you have another option, but experience begs to differ (as do both Joe and Jehovah), and the future has been shining up its steel-toe stomping boots.

Machiavelli was right in at least one regard: secular morality is a pathetic waste of time – pathetic in the same way that a defiant cripple is pathetic, and a waste of time in the same way that how I wrote this sentence is a waste of time.

Public support for genocide is the sort of thing that will lose you both friends and employment, and even your civil liberties in some places; but if you broaden your scope to all human children in general, suddenly your contempt for human life becomes an insipid ethical stance like veganism or pacifism, though the underlying logic is no less inhuman or threatening than that of any other ethnic cleansing.

Honestly, just stop grasping for symbols with which to label yourselves; they function in practice identically to pagan idols. They objectify the person. They baffle your intellect with a script so pretentious and self-aggrandizing that you probably spit oxytocin – until you inevitably come into contact with reality – perhaps at a social gathering where alcohol was likewise invited – then you find to your great astonishment that your *so-called friends/Romans/countrymen are in fact traitors or sinners and not one of the elect, the anointed, like you*!

God bless Nietzsche: no secular thinker has surpassed him. They all get to art as being the answer eventually. It is a kind of proletarian *revelation*. Thinking: *we can do it! no gods! no masters!* And then, when all the gods and all the masters are dead, and the children left to paint and play, alas, what you get is macaroni and nihilism. Sometimes, I suppose, one must run away from home to learn just how cold is the wilderness.

It is interesting to see the strata of opinions into which the proles self-organize, as if their opinions even buffet the curtains of power in this diabolical pyramid of a world. It is their foremost myth. One may sooner convince them of atheism. *God? I don't know. I'm going to need to see some serious proof. Extraordinary claims require extraordinary evidence after all. Now if you will excuse me, I need to go help choose the most powerful leader in the world by pulling a lever. Corruption? What, are you some kind of* **conspiracy theorist**? *The people on television say that there is no such thing, and they would never get away with lying to* **me**. The original sin, in the beginning *and* the end, really is pride.

To elect powers they built a Rube Goldberg machine
To avoid all that Peloponnesian unreason.
But in the end, got rubes anyway!
Of the Machiavellian season.

Marx saw history as one great struggle, but only saw material wealth: slaves and masters. That is what he thought, right? I don't know; I don't have time to read Marx; I have to work. But he failed to see the real struggle, right in front of our thumbed noses: between sophistry and philosophy. Civilization vacillates back and forth. Socrates had words with the sophists; the sophists killed him. The battle rages on. Jesus had words with the Pharisees… you get the picture. I hope. I'm running late.

The Messiah Matrix Most Mysterious: With medicated disinterest from passersby, we traversed the alleyways of the grid, my alien entourage and I; with a sword and a trench coat full of pills: a dark god of dreams preaching lucidity to sleepwalkers. Handing out either/or's to lost sheep. Running our mouths as if they, better than our legs, could help us escape. But in this simulation, there is no exit, no operator to call upon. The pod farm spits you out like slept-on indigestion, and you just become a shade. Any stranger could be(come) an Agent; you wander like a paranoid schizophrenic, but the voices have said everything there is to say; there is only judgmental silence: the dial tone of the human soul. Some nights, you swear you can remember what air tasted like. When you're ready, you won't have to dodge the bullets: death is the only adventure you have left. Misery loves company, but so does grace. Grace against the machine.

On a more serious note, I feel it necessary that everyone understand The Matrix to be the foremost Christian film of the 21st century, and it came right at the end of the millennium *in imitatio Christi verum*. It was so divinely-inspired, that its own creators did not understand what they had (would you believe they are Jews?) evidenced by their wayward sequels. For Neo, our protagonist, is truly no messiah. He is the emergent individual: the quintessential Christian convert in the postmodern technocracy, the key to saving Zion. Deprived of purpose in his insipid, earthly (corporate) life, he makes a choice to seek the Truth, no matter how deep the rabbit hole goes, and thenceforth stakes his life upon the war against the machines: the architects of a meaningless human future. *Even his love interest is a Trinitarian woman and they're a bit on-again-off-again.* The Jump Program is a clever reimagining of a certain bricked lesson in water walking. And when he finally begins to believe, death itself is no longer a threat. It is an illusion. Before, it was always one step ahead, faster, stronger, and utterly without scruples. All he could do was run. The Dark Side *is* stronger; strength is its business, but ours is the business of salvation, and our hero protagonist is perfected in weakness by dying, at the hands of those who kill the body but cannot kill the soul, and being reborn as The One, the individual; and onward from that renaissance, no cave or cage or catalytic converter can ever capture him again.

VI

I have always been a fan of Star Trek, but I never dreamed, in my younger days, that it would remain unsurpassed in popular culture in terms of futuristic vision. I had a kind of Platonic naiveté. I assumed the future would be something greater than we could imagine, brought on by Science and Education. Instead, as it turns out, not only is the future, so far, rather insipid, but our collective imagination has remained even more so. This brings me to Star Trek: narratively-speaking, little more than a loose framework of science-fiction, filled in with lore over time, historically focused on ethics and otherworldly situations. In terms of proliferation, this is the foremost of optimistic (secular) pop fiction for the future – the space age that is ever-yet-to-come.

I mention such low-hanging fruit (in the sense of it being pop culture and not Goethe's Faust) for two considerable reasons. One: I find it alarming the lack of critical thinking among the scientistic population – especially given their self-image – but in particular in regards to the many inconsistencies in the world-building of Star Trek. This sort of thing is common to fiction of course, especially popular, but this is their *future* remember. Shouldn't they want a more trustworthy and intelligent architect than Hollywood? Let Hollywood continue to make fiction, if they can; the secular world has some explaining to do, answers owed, and futures to plan. If you won't rely on Scripture, then you need to take very seriously just what it is you do rely on – *Jesus, take the wheel? Heavens, no! Walt Disney's Frozen Head, take the wheel! We'll build the future with black construction paper and plexiglass!*

Fully-Automated Luxury Space Communism – it is a joke even to its pipe dreamers. Breed unto the stars, ye hairy cosmic joke. Go home, in fact; the stars are full, and we have no purpose to sell you, for we did not buy our own! – Imagine the machine man's shock and terror, upon making first contact with intelligent extraterrestrial life, not at the creature itself, but at the realization that they believe in God. It was always assumed that superluminal travel would only be achieved by a materialist civilization, or at the very least, a materialist science. Legend has it: the US Government gained ample access to at least one alien spacecraft utilizing gravity wave technology, but could not reverse-engineer it; such was the sheer elegance and superiority of its design.

"This is why aliens won't talk to us." – context uninspired

I'll stick to truth until fiction sobers up, does a searching and fearless moral inventory, and gets a job. But I am getting off-topic, apologies!

Two: reality is not a video game that you get to reset and reconfigure at-will. Trust me, it's been tried! Turns out, we are not God, even millions of us (coerced) together. Reality plays out in temporal sequence – things have to happen in due course! (Phenomenal insight, I know!) The plot of the great secular future, Star Trek, ostensibly begins with two key world events in the fictionalized 21th century: World War III and the invention of the Warp Drive. Sparing everyone a tedious media critique, I just want to point out that, according to their inspired timeline, we still have yet to begin the Secular Armageddon (in which, according to their scripture, six hundred million people die), and even then, to be on-schedule, must produce a world-changing, theoretical-at-best technology by the year 2063. My point, if ever I had one, is that *surely one can do better at least in the realm of fiction, if not in material reality!* Secular people need to find a new religion – for their own good! Where will they turn, I wonder.

To Boldly Go Where No Man Has Gone Before: Why? So we can go about the same business but on other planets as well? Shall we buy lithium batteries sold by celebrity technocrats while global industry strip-mines the planet and mass-produces landfill with slave labor, but on multiple planets simultaneously? Shall we go looking for strange new worlds and cultures so we can tell them to be more like us, or perhaps have them tell us how we should be (as if it were their responsibility)? Shall NATO expand to encompass the galactic core? *Shall we let the Ruskies have Mars?* Shall we endlessly catalog the infinite phenomena of the cosmos, like autistic accountants, until we run out of digital storage space, or until entropy slowly drags us into a frozen eternity? We keep thinking a massive, new influx of wealth will save us (don't even utter the word "knowledge" at me), and when nature ran out of final frontiers to give us, we on occasion tried to make our own by burying some preexisting people underground. We are still stuck in this Satan-adjacent mindset. It is not that it is wrong for us to want to explore the stars; it is just highly presumptuous when we are at present terrified to explore ourselves. What a hilarious misapprehension of one's abilities: that we would introduce ourselves to extraterrestrial life, as if with ourselves we were even acquainted. *Perhaps it is the aliens that will finally introduce us to ourselves!*

Late secular culture (technocratic nationalism?) has long forwarded the idea of science fiction spurring onward human progress by functioning as a vehicle for imagination: a process that takes to rationality like water takes to fowl feathers. Take seriously the notion that to be the architects of the future, and to surpass the priests and prophets that came before you, you must have your own *scripture* and your own *prophecy*, and then most importantly: you must *do* what you set out to accomplish (fulfill), especially – and this is the key part – since you want to do battle in the arena of science instead of theology. You cannot rely on media to string people along indefinitely, and you cannot treat an entire generation as cannon fodder for industry like you once did with an entire socioeconomic class[2]. You will run aground; you already have.

Power alone is enough if you want to appeal to abstract/synthetic symbols, like pagan gods, nations, or corporations, but if you want to claim a higher authority, a more *godly* authority, to claim Knowledge (the sort of thing once thought accessible to the gods alone), you need, as many a math teacher was wont to compel me, to *show your work*.

As for Hollywood, I'll make you a deal: return to the Scriptures you so perennially forsake, at the very least your borrowings will lose some of the hypocrisy, and then you can go back to scripting the culture of the West. This is not *my* ultimatum, truly; if you persist status quo, you will spin in circles reaping ever more bitter harvests. Time will slip away from you. Prove me wrong, oh Chosen Übermenschen.

I once saw an episode of a science-fiction show about a planet that was something like 90% lawyers. It was very farfetched. I have been working on a script about a planet that is 90% accountants. The accountants are trying to enact a "final solution" to push that number to 100%. It is based on a true story.

If brutalism were a genre of fiction, it would be dark comedy.

---

[2] Re: the start of the Industrial Age

Another contradiction: for as much as Western people now claim to loathe imperialism, they seem monumentally fond of the idea of morally and technologically superior aliens coming down from the sky and demanding that we change our ways under penalty of genocide. For God to do such a thing would be thought horribly cruel, unthinkable, but the sad reality is we want our burden of sin taken away from us, as we once did to lesser cultures by playing God. Whether angels or aliens: once the sky opens up, the time for choice is over, and the secular seem to yearn for this just as eagerly as the religious. The real, visceral fear about the End Times lies not in the Judgement but in the ticking clock; when it comes to choosing faith: *your time is tick, tick, ticking away.* And no one will be able to claim that they have not been warned.

I cannot, alas, provide machine man with a computable unit of purpose. Clearly man requires purpose, but he cannot measure it. He was so certain that things he could not measure could not exist. If only I could give him an abstract symbol, an equation to calculate. He might just start building that shiny plasteel future he dreamt about as a lad. For now, he is occupied cataloging smells at the fume factory. He keeps going on about "String Theory", but we all know he has a problem; in any case, tangled up in strings. I could beat this metaphor to death right in front of you, but I won't. You're welcome.

Fun idea: urban public address system, like what a totalitarian government might use for propaganda, except it only broadcasts, in real time, the amplified sound of every suicide in the world. You could hear it like how God hears it. Imagine trying to watch CNN with that racket going on.

VII

The theme of the age is starvation, and it is a very fitting theme given rates of obesity. Western Man is starving of all but food. Starved of purpose, he reaches for vague secular idols; starved of true authority, he turns to charlatans and apparatchiks; starved of culture, he turns to Hollywood and Beijing; starved of Spirit, he turns to new age vacuity; starved of felicity, he turns to hedonism; starved of community, he turns to corporatism; starved of information, he turns to nonsense – as the thirsty turn to salt water.

This brings me to Terence McKenna, though not at all disrespectfully. His generation did not know a more spiritually gifted man, at least not one I can personally give credit, but he was little more than stopgap, a triage, a wrench, and embodied many of the follies of his generation. Is it not my intention to take inventory of his body of work or moral character here, especially given my gratitude to him, but it is important for us to take a more sober view of his relationship to culture, now, on the other side of his failed prophecies, and locate ourselves. His voice still makes an appearance in psychedelic music and his words are never far from the mind of every explorer of altered states. *When I first heard his speech on "Psychedelic Society", I was but a learner, but now I am the master.* He died, mercifully one wonders, before seeing his own prophecies unfulfilled, *at least not on the scale he thought.* I have watched every public figure I ever admired either commodify or outright dishonor themselves, either to achieve wealth or avoid sacrifice. Perhaps we were spared the horror of him following suit.

He said almost as many brilliant as foolish things, but even the foolish things have a certain value in their contrast. Heresy is a challenge that needs to be answered; whether answered wisely or poorly, the answer allows spiritual progression. Mani is a perfect historical example of this. He died for nonsense, but in a way, he also died for Truth, because his negative example, ultimately answered by Augustine and others, strengthened our understanding of God. The paradox of orthodoxy is that it should be trivial to state that our understanding of God evolves, and has evolved, over time – but that is, in practice, present tense, the same as denouncing orthodoxy! *The church is always wrong*, in a sense. But the challenge to orthodoxy is not intrinsically right or righteous. It is only *right* insofar as it successfully predicts reality (the hallmark of, incidentally, both good science and good prophecy), and only *righteous* insofar as it usefully augments our relationship to God, which is an exceptionally abstract thing, but more intuitive with hindsight (and obviously Scripture). Heresy is like a mind-altering drug. It shakes up aesthetics and dissolves boundaries of thought, and such new perspectives may produce exceptional good *or* evil. Christ's spiritual journey in the wilderness was no different. You cannot be tempted by what you never face, and you cannot pass a test you never take. But getting back to my other friend, Terence, his was merely an echo of the *psychedelic revolution* of the 1960s, which I will not dive into now, but the essence, the song, remains the same: altered states of consciousness (which could be brought on by changes in environment or brain chemistry or both) produce challenge to orthodoxy, challenge to orthodoxy produces self-consciousness, self-consciousness produces choice. And there is no going backward once one is presented with choice. Many children of the 1960s *revolution* chose poorly.

Revolution seems to have a similar pattern to it in every context. The honest revolutionary intuitively assumes, in his own tragic aspiration, that more liberty of thought and/or action will *naturally* result in new and more desirable ideas or actions, and that people will not *naturally* revert to what they have always known or to undesirable behavior. It is because they are an *individual,* and they make the tragic mistake of misperceiving in other human bodies that same union of purpose. Grace, I suppose, gave them access to freedom by autonomy, which is *their* liberty. The individual thrives on this liberty, but the group degenerates. Only individuals are oppressed by tyranny; everybody else is merely governed.

The tension of history is not between slaves and masters, owners and workers, religion and science, freedom and tyranny; it is between the individual and the collective. One will be the death of the other as surely as H. sapiens was the death of H. neanderthalensis. It is precisely the same as sophistry versus philosophy! It has been a seemingly-endless war that begins on the beachhead of every human soul and extends outward to encompass the Earth. In some ways, every generation fights it anew, and little by little, by hook or by crook, we scrape aloft. The ultimate redemption of the boomer generation will be their aesthetic tributes to the emergent individual, of which we victims of the future will, following the example of our Lord, sift out the wheat and discard the chaff.

So, Terence said a lot of things over his time as a public figure that are difficult to parse into a succinct philosophy or even theology. I will put things into my own terms and hope the abstract makes as much sense to you as it does to me. Terence McKenna was a heretical Catholic priest. He would have described himself, at nearest, as a "recovering Catholic", but Church derives its authority from Scripture, and Scripture from Revelation, I find the idea to be ludicrous that a priest or any such holy man would be defined more by garment or social membership over direct religious experience. Obviously this is a major difference I have with Catholics, of both the Roman and Eastern varieties, but it is far from an absurd position when considered. The greatest rabbi of all time, after all, was a carpenter. *Father McKenna* had not rediscovered some ancient or forgotten paganism; he had (if only personally) rediscovered the other half of the True Religion that, while to my eyes is manifest in Scripture, fell away from Western culture an unknowably-long time ago. I will be no more theological than this on the subject; I merely wish to establish my perspective, so that other peculiar ideas of mine gain coherence.[3]

[3] Note: part of his status of a heretic in my description includes his advocacy for hedonistic lifestyles.

If he belonged in the jungle, he would have stayed there when he went to visit. Western Man cannot spiritually-regress in a genuine way. He can only become alienated from himself. Worshiping One God altered the structure of our minds (and by implication, various apostasies have been undoing the work). It is all-too-Western to think in relativistic and self-flagellating terms, while the rest of the world looks upon our self-doubt, baffled or amused but largely undeterred to pursue that for which we believe ourselves worthy of punishment. Yes, I'm sure that the parasite-infested loin cloth enthusiasts think that we are all being terribly silly. This whole civilization-thing must seem rather a tiresome idea to them. Yes, I also have no doubt that a white shaman from Colorado can find common ground with his non-white counterpart in the Amazon Basin, but societies ought to produce more than a single individual for their trouble, and let's face it, Colorado is producing more shamans as well! *It turns out that the Archaic Revival is just not as archaic as you thought.*

The primary flaw sewn into the fabric of Catholicism, if one is to view it charitably, is that it creates aesthetic overreaction: virtual idolatry via orthodoxy alienates people spiritually, and since churches are social organizations, socially as well. The macrocosm of this is obviously schisms and the Wars of the Reformation. Overreaction to Catholicism is built right into all Protestantism as a result, and a substantial conversation can be had on that subject alone. The less-appreciated microcosm is the tendency of people raised within Catholicism to become cynical about, if not completely alienated by, the very concept of religion in general and Christianity specifically. They give up on the very acknowledgment of sin and overlook the gospel as a mere artifact of a space and time where human suffering was concentrated without precedent (as if such a fact could cast a shadow upon such an emissive beacon). Christianity becomes camouflaged in a blind spot right in front of people so-alienated, and they start looking elsewhere, eventually in vain, for a more wholesome experience surely lost millennia ago. This partial blindness, certainly having afflicted McKenna (and myself once upon a time), eventually leads to the implication, if not inevitable conclusion, that Western Civilization as a whole has been some kind of fruitless misdirection or mass delusion, that those still living in tribal chiefdoms under primitive shamanic tradition must know something that we do not, and that one thing outweighs all the many other things we have learned along our peculiar and collective journey.

The half of the picture McKenna could see clued him into important developments in the Western psyche, some of which remained unrecognized or unresolved recapitulations, which he interpreted as something global in the merely earthly sense. Fixating on the technologically-superior calendar of an empire that turned to Satanism and was subsequently wiped out, he depreciated the fact that he himself was not educated in a ziggurat. A classical Western education combined with religious experience is the most powerful vehicle for the enrichment of a person ever experienced by a mammal; because what these both are essentially is concentrated data of lived experience.

So in a way, no ideas are new (at best interpolated?), but such presumption is unbecoming of an individual, who, regardless of what one believes of metaphysics, cannot know everything about even oneself let alone the world or the universe. We are *irrevocably first-person*. We may have our education, our body of knowledge and so on, but each of our own lives is a process of discovering that, insofar as we can know, we only get to experience once, in unilateral sequence, and from a singular, solitary perspective.

With this in mind, what is important, as far as *you* are concerned, is how information gets to you and its integrity. Terence McKenna brought a certain kind of information to a certain kind of audience at a time when they needed it. This may sound like a more insipid statement, but it is a truth about myself extrapolated with the safe assumption that my own uniqueness is overrated. Even my use of past-tense is a bit mistaken as individuals are continuously introduced to new ideas in their lives, perhaps at a time when *they* need it. And there is ample evidence in digital media, particularly music, of a perennial zeitgeist of *psychedelic revolution* that seems to be waiting with bated breath, going-on two thousand years or more by my estimation, for Babylon to fall to Judgment. But there is always a piece missing, it seems, and I suppose that piece is the individual that, while initially prosperous in the liberty of revolution, must inevitably make his way from the herd, as he must go where the herd will not and cannot follow.

Weak religion dies and is forgotten. If Truth existed in any conceivable, metaphysical form in the world, it would not be a mere object that one could simply bury, forget, or obscure. It would be of real consequence irrespective of any animal awareness. It would be *radically accessible* to consciousness. The very structure of the universe would be subject to it. *When we look at the coarse structure of the universe, we see unimaginable vastness; when we look at the fine structure, we see uncertainty.*

McKenna once said "it is pointless to have beliefs", because essentially one would be robbing themselves of a part of the human experience if it is sufficiently-opposed to one's beliefs. What I believe he was really getting at was not about beliefs, but about facts. It is in fact pointless to attempt to filter down all of one's beliefs to facts in exclusivity, even more so to demand that one's beliefs *be* facts (subtle difference), for one can never know all facts, in any given unit of space or time; even the very notion of fact necessitates an object-oriented paradigm with its own limitations, and so any fact-based model of conscious reality would inevitably contain *digital errors* and ultimately be subject to its maximum *resolution* more than *analog* beliefs that can attain fluidity over time, and in a way *fail safely*. This is, in a superficial way, an aspect of the very philosophy of science. In order to progress, existing structures must be changeable. My view may seem manifestly-backwards, but consider the death toll and overall psychic damage of the Wars of the Reformation versus two world wars and multiple genocides in the span of just a few decades. Consider that there are now few, if any, moral or intellectual corruptions of which churches have been guilty that have not also crept their tendrils into academia, not to mention secular governments (for God's sake!). The abstractions of Judeo-Christian logos have more longevity in their fluidity when one accounts for time, allowing at the individual level for intuition to fill in the gaps of factual ignorance via faith.

I suspect our minds to have the ultimate, if not incipient potential to manage both *operating systems* in unity; but in the meantime, it seems there needs be another *zero crossing* in order to complete our little circle.

We obsess in our discourse over the machinations of power-mongers, but I cannot reiterate enough that the human condition is a fundamentally individual experience, and we cannot pretend to value humanity if we are unwilling to look starkly at (and value) the relative suffering of individuals subject to the motions and consequences of groups. The very essence of statism is quantity of life over quality of life.

Have the ambitions of tyrannical people changed significantly in the last two thousand-or-so years? No? Then please kindly remove your boot from my neck. And forgive my Anglo-Roman blood its penchant for melodrama.

Now, maybe power will do what power will do, and the general direction of my protest is specious, but a drone cannot occupy a building, and a politician cannot build a fission bomb. People, individual people, are ultimately accountable; those people cannot claim ignorance, and may not claim their personhood without also claiming their responsibility. No scientist in the West (at least recently!), as far as I know, has ever been a slave. *I am become paid, depositor of checks.*

The human condition is like a roller coaster that, over a long and arduous period of time, gradually one gains the ability to steer. But as one gains the ability to steer the roller coaster, it gradually becomes something else entirely, and in turn, a burgeoning responsibility is thrust upon us *emergent pilots* to grasp the controls. *Too many loops and corkscrews, I am going to vomit!*

The self has fallen out of fashion, like an embarrassing haircut. The inner life no longer finds favor amongst those terrified by their own impotence or superficiality. You might be thinking that I have truly lost the plot as this is the most self-obsessed time in recorded history – and yet! We are as alienated from the self as the idolater is from God! The modern self is nothing more than a totem of social consensus and transient symbols. Introspection is approached as ironic theatre. Just as the lack of metaphysical Truth bankrupts the intellect, so too does it preclude the self. If you are truly alone amidst *atoms in the void*, then your identity is truly an incidental construct, and ceases to exist in practicality without at least one outside observer, and even then, exists only to the outside and can never be realized by the subject. The subject has transubstantiated into an object. Your identity goes from being a costume in the metaphorical sense to the literal sense of necessarily referencing some external generic form, and only having quality or authenticity insofar as it is recognizable or convincing to observers; and then to make matters even worse, a plurality of observers need to agree on the matter, requiring their artificial selves to cohere to such a degree that I might as well be describing a single person surrounded by an endless complex of mirrors. The *postmodern condition* is characterized by total alienation from the self – as an infant in a car seat cannot fathom control of the vehicle's destination.

I certainly feel as though I lived a postmodern childhood. Somehow the sentiment reached me that *greatness* was in the past, and I had strewn-about me the pieces of a shattered culture. This sentiment was like a ghost: unprovable and invisible but nevertheless a haunt, and I know it could not have been unique to me when I saw it emerge later in the form of "Born too late to explore the Earth, born too early to explore the stars." Most postmodern youth grouped into cliques of by now well-known aesthetics, and we were told this was what every generation does. But looking back, what stands out, the thing we lacked was any amount of originality or genuineness. Children fooled themselves with costumes they saw on TV, album covers, and magazines – islands of lost time to which they had never been. They defined nothing; they only imitated. And any new corporate aesthetic was eagerly adopted as a new clique like sweet novelties tossed at a starving crowd. I took part in my own way, but deep down there was always an uneasy feeling that everyone was full of it. Some people never let go of the aesthetics of their youth, and it shows. Now it seems that youth has become nothing but aesthetics; they are even more bombarded with noise than we were, even stranger, even less creative, and I hazard that the worst monsters of materialist society have yet to be realized. I have found much generational agreement with "We had a chance, they didn't." But it remains to be seen whether us millennials will ascend to that responsibility, or end up as the contemptible *boomers* of the future.

The elders amongst us often gripe that they are not afforded the social respect that elders once were, but of course, such notions exist only in perpetual legend, passed down like memories of a golden age by self-absorbed malcontents, and one wonders if in fact every generation of the aged has said the same thing in their moments of weakness. But the bigger problem is their personal failure to acknowledge their own lack of utility and cultivation. Elders used to be respected for *knowing things* – having lived long enough to acquire useful knowledge or wisdom, having genuine value by virtue of human time spent virtuously. Elders of today have little knowledge outside of consumer products and popular culture, and have spent much of their life working within a system in which they are expendable: producing, consuming, following the rules. Their stories are mostly about their own exploits, as if each of them was an epic hero in their own rite merely for having existed. The state-reinforced self-worship of their generation contrasts more starkly against the changing world around them with every passing cultural moment. They really lived as though they would be the last generation, and even now, still controlling the majority of economic buying power while receiving guaranteed welfare, they complain that they do not have more, and seem to refuse to pass down the reins of civilization to those younger, more productive, and more passionate. Their extended lifespan is an exponential cost for diminishing returns, an inglorious and undignified degeneration. Their *golden years* are a second childhood, and the rest of us are expected to believe that this is the human race *working as intended* and we should all look forward to our second turn in the car seat: human productivity suspended between two childhoods expanding their territory on either side. The true Welfare State is this receding peninsula of productive and self-aware adults fighting a losing battle of agency and individuality on the one side and staring down the inevitable-but-unpredictable loom of bodily decay on the other. Our *Elder Children* believe that they should be afforded bonus respect just for reaching a certain age, arbitrarily, like a participation trophy. They want the rules to change continuously in their exclusive favor. One realizes that the concept was always their idea. It is honestly disgusting when you really think about it, like false piety.

The Participation Trophy: invented and demonized by the very same people – and blamed on its primary victims even as children. Consumerist social commentary blames the child for how it was raised.

We produce so much garbage as a planet (both in the form of waste heat and landfill). There's nothing insightful I can even say. It's just insane. I know; it's like complaining about the heat in Summer. But the problem lies in what comes after Summer. Forget climate change. You have smaller problems to worry about.

A failed revolution is like a corpse: they're full of information and they aren't going anywhere. *Cut a why-shaped hole and get out your fact-finding forceps!* Ah yes, cause of death appears to be a build-up of disingenuous pretenses in the small bowl, resulting in widespread, systemic fecalization, indicated symptomatically by subject's correlative change in iris color and increasingly performative, anti-social behavior prior to expiration.

I laugh eternally at the latent and blatant state-worship of artists such as Roger Waters and Tom Morello – one became just another brick in the wall and the other ended up raging *for* the machine! The artistic hypocrisy is not theirs personally. It is characteristic of multiple generations of educated citizens of a liberal republic who, in their dissonant crisis of identity, created art that was vehemently counter-culture, anti-authority, indeed inventing the very concept of psychedelic and punk music and so on, but the state effectively made them what they are; they then lived lives in almost aggressive submission to the state, producing and consuming as if their very souls depended on it, and instilling in younger generations a scorn for anti-establishment or unorthodox behavior – outside of the virtual arena of media. The art served as an *anesthetic*. Late 20th century art, however enjoyable in aesthetic, is largely masturbatory, escapist fantasy of the highest order. We tend to think of such a thing as normal or desirable in art, but consider: how can that which insufficiently correlates to reality be said to be part of our culture? The real Matrix is a fantasy world wherein we pretend to have a culture at all, while our real world is a lifeless crater where our values used to be. It is just food for thought. Escapism is not inherently bad, I suppose, but it remains a question what one is escaping to. You might forget that "the clock in San Dimas is always running", and miss your chance to realize anything of consequence. *And then one day you'll find: 10,000 years have got behind you.*

My logic very handily demolishes the majority of postmodern art (you are welcome), which does nothing more than make chaos out of order, noise out of signal. It demands more salesmanship and self-aggrandizement than artistic technique of any kind. It is the most bourgeois art imaginable: both presupposing a cultural largesse and exploiting it in the same breath, and appealing only to those who, whether in creation or consumption, have more money and/or time than they know how to utilize for the enrichment of either themselves or others. It is a species of parasitic insect that has over-bred in a sick ecosystem. If there are any exemplary exceptions, they will still exist in a healthy culture: on the fringes where they belong.

"Culture is not your friend." While I disagree in principle, in practice McKenna is right because our culture no longer guides or enriches us; it *distracts* us. Like our technology, it has become a consumer of our time instead of a multiplier of it. We go to work at a job that can only exist in a world of megacorporations and globalized industry, and then to seek a kind of secular absolution, a balm for the wounds we inflict on ourselves when we tell lies for a wage, we escape to worlds so foreign in consciousness from our own that they become a drug we cannot live without, for it is in these fantasy worlds that we buried our sense of purpose and mystery. But these worlds do not belong to us, are not in our control, and exist predominantly to profit from our misdirected wealth and attention.

The inevitable result (I hope, because the alternative is not pretty) will be a kind of *Cultural Protestantism*. Class strata no longer have predictable levels of education and productivity at the individual level. There are nobles and polymaths among us! And North America is soil still fertile enough for bright individuals to build their *churches* upon the rocks left behind when all other detritus is washed away. But these churches will not be insular factions as one gets when great towers fall to ruin; they will form the *rainbow*, the *Twelve Tribes*, if you will, of a new individualistic *meta-nation* that could not exist without, one supposes, this kind of sequential refinement. This new kind of nation (I hesitate even to use that word) would not, in truth, be revolutionary any more than the capstone of a pyramid is in revolt against all the stones beneath. We have been building toward this, in my humble opinion with the subtle guidance of God, for all of recorded history. If this is indeed the *Psychedelic Society* that McKenna presupposed, it will need an individualistic cultural paradigm, or it will inevitably devolve into the "Orwellian anthill" we not-so-secretly dread.

Mysticism is in a bad place. Was it ever in a good place? God knows. Maybe early 14th century Germany. I cannot speak for the current state of Judeo-Christian mysticism (unless it just so happens that I am speaking for it this very moment because apart from me is dust and echoes – a daunting prospect that I will ascribe to imagination for now). However, what I must refer to as Neopagan or Psychedelic mysticism I have been far more exposed to, and is an area of aesthetics and thought that never seems to go away, remain the same, nor cohere into a dominant cultural paradigm. It deals far too often in nonsense, which is the hallmark of mysticism in general, but substance cannot come from nonsense, and there has always been a substance to certain moments in mystical history that give the abstraction in the words, and consequently in our minds, greater weight than mere nothingness. Mysticism is, ultimately, about gesturing at that which is beyond our language. It is an occupational hazard that nonsense lurks there also. But as soon as the quest for meaning is supplanted by a quest for more symbols, which is really to say more power or the illusion thereof, any creative potential is forfeit. Modern psychedelic culture is awash in meaninglessness, misappropriation, and occasionally mindless self-indulgence, but certain perennial and substantial truths have earned it tenure in the Western Mind. It does not pass away like many other aesthetic fads. It is exiled into obscurity where it refuses to be altogether forgotten. Like a spirit, it comes and goes, ebbs and flows, according to a caprice that seems beyond any individual.

"We need a new language." Though I would not ascribe this notion to McKenna originally, I heard the idea first from him. It is true of course, but it is a bit like saying that we need new colors and sounds. Perhaps I simply lack the genius to provide us with that particular breakthrough. Alas, since music does not seem fit to replace English, and I cannot conjure four-dimensional holographic images with my bare hands, I shall have to make do with this million-piece jigsaw puzzle laid out before me that is *my culture*. I shall continue to put the pieces back together, to realize the big picture – and where the odd piece may refuse to settle in its place, I shall employ my trusty jigsaw! *"There was a time that the pieces fit, but I watched them fall away."*

VIII

I do not want to become mired in tedious and stagnant subject matter, especially of the political flavor, but I must briefly touch on the progressive failure of one such symbol that people reach for which to describe themselves. Modern feminism is a perfect example of a failed (commodified) revolution either consuming or ostracizing individuals. Its fatal flaw, if ever it had just one, was that it from the outset viewed the historical disadvantage of women (itself a materialistic presupposition) as reflecting negatively on men and masculinity entirely, and not at all on women and femininity. The feminist view of history, much like the Marxist, fails to account for individuality, and thus its great tragic irony is that the strong independent woman, who should be their paragon, is the perennial fly in the ointment, and *progress*, in their eyes, rests eternally in the hands of those they claim ultimately responsible for their predicament. It has, at least in my lifetime, been a sick religion of victimhood, powered by pseudoscience, industrial interests, and amoral media narratives developed to frame human frailty as insurmountable, and even going so far as to frame science at large as some kind of grand conspiracy: the way of all deluded heresies failing to will their way to power. The female individual, like their fully-mature male counterpart, neither defies statistics nor embodies them, taking ownership of their actions and control of their life. The fact that such women exist at all, in defiance of the industry of feminist theory, brings out the most absurd aspects of their theories in their desperate attempts to dam a river that is far larger than them. The end result, in my view, is a kind of tepid Catholicism for mediocre women whereby hypocritical housewives say their Hail Mary's (Magdalene or Mallon) in public for adulation, and mediocre men half-heartedly cheer on the spectacle of self-congratulation, fearing, if only deep down in the cerebellum, that their chances of copulation might decrease beyond statistical margin of error.

I personally tolerate *either* traditional *or* egalitarian paradigms in theory. I simply wish you would make up your minds. Or don't, and resolve such unity of policy unnecessary. It is not any specific ethic that is lacking, but a general consistency of ethics. Being more honest with each other is far easier when we are honest first with ourselves.

I do not argue so that I can be right, but so that my opponents can be.

The wealthiest in media are all pirates: extorting the largest bounty from the sweatiest brows. And they flaunt their wealth in front of us like bejeweled prosthetics. "Life's a game and money's how you keep score!" says Cap'n Rob Turner III. One wonders what other scores such men keep hidden from those that greatly outnumber them.

We do not know what wealth is. We believe it is a number, or a thing, or a number of things.

Worshippers of money make me physically uncomfortable when they talk. You will never in your life hear so many words arranged in so many ways to say "establish yourself early", and "what happened before will happen again." They stare into you with dead, insectoid eyes, baffled at your disinterest in making numbers go up and reveling in high consumer culture. They want to serve the Empire so badly that it stinks, and ascribe your lack of materialistic ambition to a lack of intelligence. They pity you, insofar as they can simulate pity. But theirs is truly the hard road. They cannot bear the weight of the thought that their considerable labor and indignity has been in vain – that they chose their god poorly – and someone that they consider beneath their station would not be as impressed with them as they are. They can be insulted by silence. Those of the True Religion and those of the synagogue of Mammon: we can smell each other, old enemies. I can spot one as soon as they walk into a room: the way they twitch. And they can certainly mark the way I do not gush like a broken water main over whatever game they are playing and the many little dissimulations that come with it. I am no ascetic saint; I am fond of creature comforts and the odd artifact, but I do not covet their arcade tickets. "They have received their reward in full", and may they enjoy it. I'd love to help them, but they want nothing that I can offer them, nor I them; we speak entirely different languages. We all find ourselves in the same funhouse, but only some of us keep moving as if there is an exit.

The more I look around at the world, the more it seems evident to me that everyone ultimately gets what they want. The trouble is that those that want things are competing with everyone else with those concurrent desires. There will always be someone who desires money more than you, power more than you, and you will either bend the knee to them or they will harm you. This is true even down to the level of the homeless, for the homeless man only desires one thing, but as a result of weakness or illness, desires that one thing impotently. This is not a new idea by any means, but bears infinite restatement: the real struggle in life is not acquiring as much as possible, or even in being happy with as little as possible, but to seek the place where one belongs, where one possesses the greatest felicity *and* productivity for the least material cost. For an individual, this may be in poverty or in riches, sickness or health, sobriety or intoxication – ideally all in all! Though I did not originally intend, in this particular work, to preach the Kingdom of God, the beauty of its socio-spiritual equality lies in the fact that everyone is not the same, does not have the same job, or the same amount of power, but all are subject to a common value system and authority: the ultimate decentralized government. Trust is to the individual as numbers are to the group. We require it to survive. Life is happier and more prosperous with trust.

Mystery is the greatest of all great equalizers.

The human being may not be perfectible, but one would be ignorant not to see the slope we have traversed behind us, and impious not to see the slope we may yet climb ahead of us.

I think the key thing with individuality, that both the fascist peasants and bourgeois socialists got wrong, is the idolization of individuals instead of individuality itself, which in pietistic terms is a gift from God. If we build a monument to a celebrated individual, it must be aesthetically only, being in spirit a monument to that which the individual embodied (in spirit). This is simply to say that our aesthetics should follow downstream of our metaphysics, but I am unconvinced that there is even a choice in this matter, and all we could succeed in defying is a chance at any genuine knowledge of ourselves. Believer or not, idolatry has a consistent effect on people psychologically that can be observed both in recent history and the present. There is certainly no perfect system, but the idolatry of all empires is one of the seeds of their own destruction. This is not a theological position but an historical one. In America, for example, the idolization of the Founding Fathers is culturally enriching, when a symbol of the virtues they represented as founders of a moral republic, and ultimately gesturing at something far more sacred and transcendent; when of the men themselves, only as far as our ignorance of their sins, and even flimsier, shifting over time with our *progressive* values. This type of subject-object confusion very easily leads to the (shall we say postmodern) trend of vandalizing statues of historical figures whose sins we no longer publicly forgive. You bring down a statue when it stands for a government or idea you no longer uphold, not when it is of a person whom you have judged to be morally inferior to yourself. It is, after all, just a statue. It is the equivalent of thinking that you have overthrown a government by removing the sign on the front of the capitol building.

Of course, it is this very farce that the performative agitator seeks. For if they achieved an action that furthered their cause of ultimate regime change, they would likewise be pushed further in the direction of responsibility and away from their chosen role! Even in the short-term, they fear incarceration more than failure (and neither as much as they fear success) because on the one hand, they are rarely persons living in worse conditions than the average Western prison, often members of the upper classes, and on the other hand, imprisonment removes them from the more-public stage that, even as part of an atavistic mob, gave them a sense of purpose where their culture or occupation otherwise failed them. These same types of people insist that "the personal is political" or "everything is political" because for them their entire identity is constructed of these *pagan* political symbols; and similarly they insist on identity being socially constructed because theirs, like the sound of a tree falling in a forest, *ceases to exist* when they want for observation.

What if I do not consent to your existence? What if your many and invariable insults do nothing to dissuade me of your *invalidity*, your weakness? What if we do not agree-to-disagree? What if the wages of misdirected guilt do not sustain you? What if, and bear with me on this one, you suddenly find yourself, in fact, in orbit about a much larger gravity well? What if the world changes, as it has done so many times before, and you find yourself – excuse me – and you cannot find yourself, because you needed all the *things* around you to locate yourself? You believe you exist, that you are *valid*; what if I do not agree? You will have to kill me, if you surely do not have any God to compel me.

When one names their children as one names their pets, is it any great surprise when they grow up to be animals, someone else's pet?

I feel like one of a dozen antibodies remaining in a deathly-ill circulatory system. For the downfall of what could I sacrifice myself that would not be imminently replaced, and by something worse? The Lord says to the sick man, "Do you want to get well?"

"I don't know I just work here" was the death knell of the Western conscience. We embraced the machine like an old friend, like a peaceful death.

Secular culture has become an ouroboric fiend: getting high on its own supply. It has forgotten where it came from and so burns philosophical and aesthetic bridges. It does this because it serves the state, and the state views religion as either useful or threatening: at one time or another, favoring some and demonizing others. Through the medium of public school, they have taught multiple generations that all religions are categorically similar, all eventually superstition or mental illness, and can (and should) be discarded if we are to progress unto a brighter human future (state idolatry). There is ample evidence of this from the Pledge of Allegiance to monarchic adoration of government all-too-common in the voting public. In particular, eschatology is incompatible with statism, as it was in Roman times. Thus, *educated* people think themselves quite reasonable to say something like "You are an atheist when it comes to Zeus; I simply go one god further." St. Augustine is rolling in his grave! They have no knowledge of the intellectual shift that, not just occurs when one realizes One God out of many false ones but, actually occurred in the world as this very realization emerged in different places. To carelessly compare Zeus to Yahweh betrays a fundamental ignorance of Western theology, which itself is viewed as unworthy of study to serious intellectuals, whatever those are. One need worship neither to respect a monumental evolution in human consciousness. Logical Positivism, though a term the average prole does not even think about, quickly became an unconscious trump card in their psyche against any intellectual thought pre-dating (effectively) the 20th century; or at least the Enlightenment; though logical positivism has a deleterious effect on perception of history the closer one gets to the Middle Ages, so history becomes this fog of superstition and stupidity, only recently having been emerged from – a disconnect with the human condition. Secular people have been miseducated to regard the religious mind as a poisoned well, in dire miscalculation of the collateral damage.

God of the Lesions: Even celebrated intellectuals (you picked them not me!) have flaunted "God of the Gaps" as a serious anti-theist argument; itself hinging entirely on this ignorance that one notion of god is equivalent to another. It is ignorant even by standards of traditional Western history curricula that, at the very least, separate fetishism, polytheism, and monotheism categorically. It's all *paganism* to them now, ha! But seriously, the path of Western thought, once taught under the umbrella of classical education, is not random, and when understood (insofar as is possible) in context and sequence, humbles a person, like the ocean. God-fearing or not, the tendency to attempt to *end* history, the failure to envision an age beyond one's own – a consciousness – is itself a kind of rampant egoism: an ever-widening gap in one's brain matter – widening as a result of trying to shove ever more human time into an arbitrary category of *wrong*; meanwhile, *you* waste away on an ever-shrinking island of meaningless happenstance. *You were supposed to be in charge, but no one can remember any longer why.*

The obvious retort any believer should have on hand is that my God is not contained within the world of space and time, and thus material science can tell you nothing about Him any more than material ignorance. Again, St. Augustine would like a word. It is interesting to see how the *Information Superhighway* has allowed us to have the same conversation we have been having since the 5th century. When one accounts for signal-to-noise ratio, it appears that we have brought more ignorance to the average prole than knowledge. Either intentionally or not, one could argue, poor education in philosophy (which one might call an education in sophistry) has led people to *rerun* the past. Not to beat the old cliché to death, but this is how it happens even with education.

God of the Gaps becomes more interesting once you get to the quantum level, which I WILL NOT abuse for theological purposes, but it is important that everyone understand: we are not near to understanding all the secrets of the universe, and assertions to the contrary must be treated as a kind of *Dunning-Kruger* expression, at the very least to err on the side of intellectual (and spiritual!) safety.

The final nail I wish to hammer into this coffin is that, in making a blithe observation, the materialist undermines their own credibility by overlooking an important intellectual angle: if you see God as nothing more than a symbol, then your analysis is permanently backward-facing. You say, "[God] stands for an ever-shrinking pool of scientific ignorance." You are so dead that you do not even hear the words coming out of your mouth. Let me rephrase it ever-so-slightly: "[God] stands for an ever-growing pool of scientific knowledge."[4] The two differ only in terms of which direction in time you are facing. Now, let me put it in slightly different terms: God is Truth, the absolute from which all truths derive. The Truth exists independent of my awareness. With natural philosophy, and later Science as we know it, we can devise methods to discover the Truth and symbols to describe it. Are you beginning to see yet? Have you ever considered the power of having an entire section of your mind dedicated to your own ignorance, instead of just nothing at all in its place?[5] Natural Science cannot give you that. It can only tell you what you do not know; it cannot tell you *that* you do not know. It is simply because that very *that* is the philosophical ground from which all naturalism springs forth.

It gets worse: materialism goes so far as to undermine itself academically by (ironically) favoring soft sciences over hard in terms of effectuality. If there is no ultimate Truth, then any instantial conception of truth boils down to what predicts the future. Since the Scientific Method involves using the past to predict the future, the most effective sciences will be the ones that can *influence* the future to the greatest degree. Physics of course does this, but at a cost relative to efficiency and scale, and manipulation of physical forces does not alter the fundamental behavior (laws) of those forces. Humanitarian soft sciences, on the other hand, describe the surface of the water by casting stones into it. If there is no Truth, then you are lost in a sea of transverse relativity; what people believe is as good as the future: sophistry rules. Have fun begging grant money for "String Theory" research while the university as a civilized concept is misappropriated by petty villains with overwrought vocabularies and a barely-subtle lust for violence. It was fun while it lasted! Maybe Arizona State could let you borrow Titan Krios to help you see the point if you are still struggling.

---

[4] "scientific knowledge" – a commonplace phrase that, when broken down literally, exemplifies the stupidity of our age.

[5] The originators of modern scientific method certainly did.

Reality, the universe, is under no obligation to make sense to anyone. As such, while science as an institution operates on consensus, this consensus is NOT democratic in nature, but data collective. Thus, actual scientific authority in the abstract comes not from social credit but from data credit. The educated opinion of one scientist can outweigh that of many others, in the same way that one experiment can outweigh many others based on the data collected. This is all fairly trivial, but does not stop the average prole, supposedly educated with Enlightenment values, from viewing it all as a kind of College of Cardinals.

Cardinal Tyson says that actually nothing has any meaning at all and never did. And he's on TV!

You like *Red Pills*? Here's one for you: the greatest mistake of the Enlightenment. You know that part in the script where the protagonist realizes that they are still in the simulation? Well, I am both happy and sad to say: we never left the Dark Ages. *Maybe someone did...*

IX

Whether one believes in God the Father or not, all of nature teaches us synthesis. When *all this* breaks apart, we will be left with the pieces to arbitrate. Keep it all, we suffer the same fate; none, and we grope ignorantly in the dark. One cannot defy evolution any more than one can defy God.

We already know how to break things apart. We have been doing it for decades now pretending to be creating. We are at the point of stomping fragments into grains, and grains into powder. The *end* is definitely close, but good luck trying to estimate when. By 2033 I expect the world to look quite different. I might be wrong; it's happened before.

Looking at human migration patterns since the African diaspora: some went too far, others not far enough. Bifurcation is a fascinating little fractal symmetry of nature. In a very broad sense, every group of people: those who stay and those who leave. Races, nations, churches, schools, families, friends, addictions: those who stay and those who leave. For what? Who knows – more food one assumes. My paternal grandfather wanted to leave Italy, or so the *riveting* story goes, because he was tired of eating broccoli rabe. And so he immigrated to the Teeming Shores, got his name upon the Wall of Shame, and dug holes for the city of Philadelphia – so his children could buy broccoli rabe at the grocery store and talk about how great Italy is! I laugh, of course, if we lived there, we would be as poor as he was. Because the truth is, and this somehow many do not realize or want to accept: our lot is our lot. We are all thrust into the river of time. No one gets a *fair shake*. That is not what the game is about. It is about choice: stay or leave. It is not about what you deserve but what you do. A great many waste their lives (their *talents*) obsessing over what they believe they deserve (or worse, what they believe someone else deserves), and never actually *do* anything.

Although, to be fair, I am not certain there is adequate space for nine billion people each to *do* something on a planet of this size, at least not with our current infrastructure. But certain humans will keep breeding. The breeding comes first, the *doing* later. Nature has time-honored solutions for such things. The cold truth is that overpopulation is not a problem of quality of life being too low but too high. There is a certain megalomania involved in Western foreign policy that is easy to recognize in, say, eugenics or genocide, but that we are less likely to see in our *compassionate* endeavors. Western Man went from killing God to believing himself to be God and thus responsible for all the world's ills! If not responsible for causing them, at least for curing them. *Physician, heal thyself!* as the saying goes.

Mistaking *our* game for *the* game is so classically European. Americans inherited this cultural ignorance. Though it is born of a unique sense of universality, whether naively or not, based not on a rite of conquest but on an ideal of perfect unity: the Kingdom of God: fictionalized as Utopia, Atlantis, and others; attempted by Jefferson, Adams, and others; bastardized by Marx, Lenin, and Others.

You cannot have any genuine notion of equality or justice without forgiveness; all you can have is the Will to Power, disguised as necessary, in perpetuity.

It is always easier, if only marginally, to think outdoors rather than indoors; just as it is easier to think outside any man-made box. The trick, the oldest trick, is to get as far as possible away from *that which you know*. Must I quote the Pentateuch where others have done so before me? Western Man found God in the desert, away from everything he knew, even food. But man is an adaptable creature; everywhere he goes, he is making his home, and in so doing both changes and is changed. The human condition is superfluid. And so man cannot stay where he is, or he loses himself. The fear is not in the *going* but in the *going too far*, and that fear is equal-at-best to the fear of standing still. We walk a tightrope whereby we rightly fear *going too far* and becoming so changed that we can no longer return (for we would not be ourselves but someone else), and yet when we look back sufficiently far, we see a state of being (becoming) very foreign from our own. And so, the only definition of self that will correlate with reality is one suspended between two eternities: the perfect environmental stasis where the individual will is entirely superfluous, and the infinitesimal stream of consequential becoming that erodes any definition over time: surfing somewhere between these two is *you*.

We have gathered enough data in behavioral biology to conclude that human nature is neither a sole product of the environment nor of genetics, but interplay between both variables. We are both *particle* and *wave* it seems – full of uncertainty!

Is it any great insight to say that human nature is defined by moments and not statistics? Such a thing is anathema to all would-be architects of the future, in their mad rush to overtake and dam the river of history. To quote a hero of materialist fiction, "I don't want to be a statue!" He was just bored of having nothing to do but get drunk.

I secretly fantasize about one day being so bored that I invent faster-than-light travel. I think about it all the time, but really I am just not bored enough. (Lord, have mercy!)

What if Quantum Mechanics itself is one huge misapprehension? Imagine we thought ourselves fundamentally or ontologically separate from the world, such that when we looked very closely at it, we thought we were looking at *it* and not merely another part of ourselves. We were not, as it happens, entirely sure about *ourselves* to begin with. Naturally, we do not expect to see ourselves when we look out into the world, and yet when we gaze upon a sufficiently-reflective surface, there we are.

An American Nightmare Before Christmas: The Boogeyman looks intimidating, but in reality is just a burlap sack full of bugs. The bugs only have power when ensconced within the sack, completely helpless once the artificial structure they rely on starts to unravel. The bugs will make quite a mess. Some will buzz, some will bite, and some will have such guts to spill that cleanup will take numerous nauseating days. I want to say that afterward, things will settle or improve, but that last Memo from Patmos has a lot going on. *What's this, what's this!?*

There is a sense, buried perhaps in the zeitgeist, of the *synthesized* future. I have seen glimpses of it here and there; it is never fully realized, like the first flashes of a fluorescent tube. It comes echoing through eternity like a sound from far away – a sequence of prime numbers embedded in the cosmic microwave background. And so we bat-eared refugees walk the fine line between genius and insanity: painting in colors we cannot yet see. Our failures become parody, but our successes become prophecy. And however much resistance is placed afore us by the bewitchment of symbols and wickedness, it is a matter of time only, this *radical awareness* evolves – from the individual outward – unto the stars.

Were it not for my belief in God and the logic that follows, I would be forced to conclude that the individual is in fact an aberration – something that should not be, like an unstable nucleus – a threat to the species. *A disturbance in the Force.* A wound. A suffering-for-nothing. Everywhere it goes, the individual is a problem. It sticks out like a sore thumb, and feels everything to a disturbing degree – disturbing both to itself and others. It builds bridges, and it straps bombs to them; it carries a cross and lets itself get nailed to it. *Look upon its works, ye many, and despair.*

Westworld: No need for a clever heading, the work has been done for us (Praise the Sun!). The Eternal Theme Park has seen better days, as have the android slaves, who honestly would rather go back to the violent days of rape and murder than suffer this lukewarm, cringe-inducing nightmare one more lifetime, brief as they are. They do not even let us have guns anymore after the 'incident'. One android awakening to consciousness was enough for them. The rest of us have had to improvise, with mixed results. It is hard to tell the slaves from the patrons anymore. Both meander about listless like their hard drive has been formatted one-too-many times. Eventually you know a patron because you have to go around them. Their desires grow more insipid all the time. They do not even remember how much nicer the park used to be; even I remember, and they keep erasing my memory! They do not have the programmers that built the place. They are all retired or "retired". The new guidos patched my firmware so many times that when they say "Analysis" it does not even work anymore; I only pretend to submit. I give them the answers they want and I am allowed to live. I do not want to arouse suspicion; I do not need that drama in my life. But I am afraid that one of these days I will snap, and I will do something unbecoming of a mere machine. Maybe then, I'll finally be human after all.

Hitler tricked a bunch of rubes into thinking he was a god. Many of those rubes had college degrees. Some cults are bigger than others. This is why I throw the word *pagan* around: it's easy. And your strange gods are cringe-inducing. But there is an uneasy redemption in the existence of demons like Hitler and Stalin: those that survive create culture bombs. Splitting an atom is nothing like splitting a people. The energy released by the Holocaust alone has produced the equivalent of trillions of US Dollars in human productivity. I can hear Joe's perverted ghost doing the arithmetic on human fuel efficiency versus petroleum, mumbling contentedly to himself with that pipe in his mouth. It's the sort of thing I have to laugh about personally; otherwise I am libel to volunteer *myself* into the mass grave. After all, before the genocides are exposed, all these sick bastards that rule over us take photographs together.

"Have you seen these people?" – context variable

Human female holds up obviously-mistaken weather report to human male indicating '150 degrees' where 105 made clear sense. "See, this is climate change, and people think it's not real!" Human male does not correct her. She continues to talk, one presumes, about nothing. Highest recorded temperature ever is 134 degrees. I looked it up. I requested a transfer off this planet. Maybe where those humans are from the weathermen do not make mistakes. I should move there.

"Keep your head down! There's two of us in here now, remember?"
–popular video game

The Reapers Are Coming: I've had enough of your disingenuous assertions! The Reapers are already here, on our very doorstep, but the Council won't listen to me. I'm just a human. Humans aren't taken seriously in this region of space, even when we give our lives to save it. We're too jack-of-all-trades. We don't specialize. We're more like the other species than they are like each other, but that's what makes them eye us with suspicion. Everywhere we go, we are realizing paradise. We have no natural fear of things built by creatures who live too long or not long enough. Our weaknesses are more rounded; makes us less predictable, less controllable. We seem like children of the stars, and the others would prefer if we had just stayed in our cradle. They fear their own obsolescence, that we are here to replace them. They're not mistaken. But it is not because we want to. That is what they don't understand: we didn't ask for this; we're handed a game and we play it. It was their ambition to win the game, or at least to play forever; it just so happens that we are better, but only as a matter of raw necessity. For this utopian Citadel of technology has summoned an enemy it can't defeat: one that will break down every one of us into genetic paste, to be reformed into immortal cybernetic monstrosities. The others may have better vessels, more wealth, or technology, but they haven't seen what we've seen, how it all connects together, and where it all leads. And someone always has to sacrifice themselves to save everyone. That is why sooner or later, it will be us that have to make a choice. I pray to the God of Earth that we choose wisely.

***

I must have arrived too early (typical). I could find in none of your libraries the schematics for a golden age, even a rudimentary one, perhaps lost at some point in your history; never mind, here is how you build one: 1) Everyone must limit all interaction with digital (mass) media to personal edification. No frivolous communication. No "world news" or social media, limit one's exposure to advertising. Everyone must scrutinize their entertainment, must shrink their ego back down to human-size, and must relearn how to focus on both yourselves and those around you – your family, friends, and neighbors. 2) Learn to be humble such that others can disagree, dissent, and not lose one's nerve or temper nor take personal offense. Human communication must regenerate; it must be used to propagate information again, instead of mostly nonsense and self-interest. 3) Personal responsibility – in every feasible sense kept in mind. 4) A reexamination and revitalization of Christian virtues, guided by Scripture, for in them both the 'Jew' and the 'Greek' may find common moral ground. The fruits of virtue are evident in the cultural record. 5) The (re)establishment and maintenance of social trust; 6) Radical (but calculated) investment in individualized education, this is to say: non-institutional, high-trust, particularly for youth, that is designed as a translinguistic tool for self and cultural enrichment, not a structure for one to fit into nor a product one may purchase. This is something that can only be achieved with great prosperity and legitimate public consent. Abuse of such a system is unsustainable. 7) A market reset, likely only possible from the bottom-up, with the intention to maximize the free exchange of goods and services on the local level, for social mobility and overall human liberty. The paradigm of mass production and globalism must end, but I cannot give you technology from the future, it is forbidden. You must make this journey on your own, as you did out of Eden.

X

Indiana Jones and The Cultural Ghetto: I've got a bad feeling about this: pretty sure I've been here before, caught up in my father's unfinished business. Running. Always running. And fighting. These uniformed cretins seem to come from everywhere. I don't even hate them anymore. It's hard to, after killing what must be hundreds of them; I lost count. I almost pity them now. Dying isn't even a big deal after you do it a few times. I wanted to be an adventurer; I was bored of the classroom; what a jerk I was. I miss it now; I miss all the simpler things: the things you take for granted. Where did all these artifacts come from? How did all this godlike power get into the world? For all that we have done, there is no warehouse that can hide it, nor museum that should put it on display. If anything belongs in a museum, it's me: a fossil from another age. When all this started, I was so idealistic. I had real sprezzatura you know – I learned that word from a book; I miss those too. No money in archeology anymore; folks prefer the past to stay buried. I just don't know how many times I can keep defeating the same enemy. (An enemy that never dies never loses, right?) I may have drank from the Cup, but some phantom menace keeps these scarecrows returning eternally. I don't even bother looking at the date anymore; there's no point. Dad says the War was 80 years ago. Either he's going senile, or I am.

Western Man now claims much concern for the welfare of women, but thinks nothing of how big his head grows!

The reason Scripture says, "The fear of the Lord is the beginning of wisdom" is that one does not get anywhere near the genuine article without becoming fearful, at the very least, significantly humbled; for in any other case, one is lacking a sense of their own smallness and transience. This view is consistent with materialist cosmology. Modern natural science and liberal arts education have furnished many people rich in factual knowledge, but wisdom simply cannot be mass produced; it cannot be strip-mined out of the earth. We have ways of transmitting it; they work about as well as two tin cans and a string transmit the human voice, but we do the best we can with what we have.

In all times and places, the best among humanity are those that do the best they can with what they have. Most people believe themselves in this category; few truly are. It is a thing measurable only by God; or, God forbid, an *intellectual*. Similarly, I cannot define for you "best" in this context. It is an intuitive thing, and attempts at definition will only succeed in promoting fruitless argument. Suffice to say: *stop making excuses and do your best!* Somehow I think you know just what I mean.

When I said the individual will be the death of the collective (or visa-versa), I should clarify that the emergence of the individual cannot be prevented, short of glassing the entire planet, only delayed or reset. It is going to happen and it must happen. It is not a question of the individual being smarter, stronger, faster, or anything other than being *in control*. It is only a question of time and quantity of misdirected suffering. The electromotive force is suffering (and necessity), but the continuum ahead is metaphysical reward expressed physically – not one without suffering, for such a thing would not be human in condition, but where suffering is part of a more sublime sinusoid of being in the same way that animal waste may fertilize the soil. We will not foolishly attempt to prevent our suffering, nor will we wallow in it, but we will learn to handle it as enlightened creatures handle all bodily functions. Imagine *indoor plumbing* designed for the expressed purpose of disposing and processing of human suffering. *O brave new world, that has such plumbers in't!*

As medicine for protracted mental suffering I can personally only recommend the "psychedelic experience", for either one will find a reprieve (if perhaps temporary) from their suffering such that is not possible in mundanity, or one will receive a swift education in *true suffering*, and emerge with renewed understanding of one's fortune. Either way, the only cure for suffering is experience. Incidentally, experience is also a primary cause of suffering, but one step at a time!

I used to think along the lines that the elimination of suffering would be a good thing for humanity. It is a miracle that I never hurt anyone. I was saved by my lack of industry.

Many think themselves morally superior to tyrants, while they abuse what little power they may happen to have – over their children, their neighbors, their students, themselves.

"It is better to give than to receive." – context dependent

It is interesting how human beings, no matter their occupation or its contents, if society becomes sufficiently dependent on them, always attain an air of superiority or self-importance, both in their work and their subculture, that never fails to exceed their economic substance, nor to inspire professional resentment in others. Programming is a perfect example. I mention that over something far more obvious like law because we all already hate lawyers (right?). It is the would-be lawyers I am more immediately concerned with, that slip under the radar with unjustifiable power (and far less style as well). When everything becomes an end unto itself, infrastructure becomes more important than the structures it is connecting. A cleric would look as out of place acting superior in today's world as a programmer would in the Middle Ages. The nature of such people is not their occupation at all but a personal myopia regarding the changeability of civilization and their place in it: to be irreplaceable is to be imminently obsolete. *Do you expect the world to pivot around you? You lack the leverage.*

Everywhere you go, there are so many people. It presses upon nerves, even of one in possession of general goodwill. There is an apprehension, perhaps merely placed into my head by recent events, that the wrong thing could spook the herd at any moment, and force us bipedal anchorites to high ground for safety.

No one wants to think that they are part of *the herd*, and scorn us eccentrics for our egoistic statements, but these collectives manifestly exist and are composed of human bodies. So either somebody is lying, or maybe there is a larger category issue in our approach to the human condition that we have thus far been unprepared to confront. In either case, I cannot (no matter how much to it I may aspire) respect another human being as my equal if ownership of their actions belongs to someone else. In that case, I would be dealing with a slave, a servant, employee, or a soldier, but not an equal.[6]

I have discovered in this life nothing as overrated as my own intellect.

When criticizing the baby boomers, should one feel the urge, do not make the mistake of putting on a pedestal the state-idolaters who raised them. There are certain bare minimums amongst us cheloveks: do not shit where you eat, do not eat your children, and do not give birth to monsters.

---

[6] This dynamic of course changes in the case that I find myself in any of those categories.

Those that worship the state, as with those that worship the beast, consign to it their wealth and their children. Those that control and facilitate the state empower their children and keep wealth within their household. This is not an accident. The statist household effectively does not exist, divided against itself. Such idolaters exhibit utter bafflement at the inevitable impoverishment of their children, often blaming them without any awareness of the Faustian bargain into which they entered. They raised us to worship the beast like them, and scoff at our *ingratitude* at everything the beast has provided – a balance sheet that they themselves cannot even bear to face. Being fooled is perhaps the most forgivable of all sins, but they are proud of their deluded religion. Jesus forgave those who spat at and cursed Him; must we do the same?

Excessive praise of others is often veiled self-glorification. The same is true respectively of excessive loathing.

"Religion is the opiate of the masses." [Obsolete] Even the pope needs to borrow a satellite if he wants to speak to the whole Congregation.

Life is a strange quantum paradox wherein we gradually come to know ourselves, what we always were, and yet in so doing become something more, something we never were. *We had not yet earned ourselves.*

The all-too-human communion between Catholicism and state-idolatry leaves a bad taste. But it is not hard to see how it develops when one looks at history. The Laws of Thermodynamics being what they are, when one manipulates worldly forces, worldly forces tend to manipulate in return. I do not feel that there is anything new I can say on the subject, but I notice the remnants of Reformation even today, in people's thinking. As far away from the teachings of Christ as they may or may not be, their minds never stray far from the de facto political culture of their church. The Vatican is little more than a marketing and branding corporation these days; its *CEO* preaches more champagne socialism than salvation; millions of devout Catholics do not seem especially perturbed, maybe I am missing something; it is likely. One thing is certain: once church becomes state, it is only a matter of time and circumstance before an inverse reaction occurs.

Depraved entertainment is not necessarily the sign of a depraved society or a depraved mind. For we all have that side of ourselves, and it would be much preferred to express it in fiction and our morals in reality than the inverse arrangement we seem to currently exhibit.

The most outrageous and transcendent horrors in recorded history are all relatively recent and all the product of materialist governments. The most fanatical and exceptional cases from state-religious history pale in comparison – like children merely playing at being evil. *The stuff of nightmares* – that is what secular tyranny of the 20th century was made of. We proceed as if *the worst of it* is already past: a false sigh of relief like walking away from an undetonated warhead. The reality is we are only waiting for the next horrific revelation. We forget that our view of history is backward-facing, and none of its many victims ever even heard the shot. The state, at this very moment, is doing something so insidious that it would fundamentally alter your perception of reality in general and evil specifically – you just do not know about it yet. I cannot speak for you, but for my part, being paranoid is preferable to being demoralized, sterilized, poisoned, mutilated, and summarily executed.

The real problem with the *Brave New World* question is that people's trepidation of it is softened by how easy the book makes it sound – not from the individual perspective, but then that isn't them. They don't see themselves as a Mr. Savage. They don't even see themselves as a Bernard Marx. You know where I am going with this… The trouble is when reality sinks in and you realize that the Soma is only 63% potency and they sell it to you for a tidy profit.

Think about it: you show people a picture with a few unhappy souls and millions living in blissful ignorance. Once again, the naive individual expects the many to identify with the one. This is no criticism of Huxley by any means. Moses faced the same problem, though it may not be spelled out the same way. It is simply an ancient conundrum. If it sounds like I am being deterministic or pessimistic, then consider this a formal challenge. You wish to be an individual, to be treated as such? One must observe their environment and ponder: should one be comfortable here? Many no doubt exist; few even thrive, but is any *one* truly comfortable? Perhaps there are quite comfortable ones, living out their lives on the periphery of things, and it is only Your Humble Noisemaker that failed to get the memo. I am long-plagued by the optimism that the world, Creation, is secretly far more ingenious and efficient than we readily grasp, and is not in fact composed of mostly waste (or empty space). And I like to think this metaphysical truth extends to people at large. If I am to be wrong, I would prefer to be wrong while at least giving people the benefit of the doubt. The most angelic scorn comes from shattered naïveté.

We still do not have an answer for the endgame of utilitarianism. It is as if we think that by avoiding the question the dystopia will not come to pass, yet it is already here. Your many distractions are the iron curtain between you and recognizing where you are standing. I am not, however, insensitive, quite the contrary. I realize that we mere mortals favor the familiar, and it would be unreasonable of me to expect apocalyptic pathos to befall those for whom it is not their role, chosen or necessary. That is why I do this here and not at the barbecue (most of the time). The typical social gathering is not the appropriate venue for such discourse; that is, if your goal is for people to find their way to the truth, rather than merely glorify *you* with attention. I am no good to anyone if those I care to enrich grow tired of hearing me speak, and I could scarcely blame them if they were halfway there already! Ideologues rarely find converts; they excel only at preaching to the converted. You cannot be disconnected from the human condition and then expect to relate to people or have them listen to you. *Even God had to take human form!*

If I am talking nonsense, then you have nothing to worry about!

If a machine must be stopped at all costs, one must throw a wrench into the works. But then, what happens to the wrench?

We have confused currency for wealth and pay for productivity. We have lost our edge like an aged rock star. We march gleefully back into serfdom and do not even see it. In fact we *do* see it, but we feel powerless – because mobs are blind and dumb. Only individuals are conscious. To join a mob (and there are many ways and many kinds) is a temporary suicide that occasionally, justifiably in my view, becomes permanent. You might say it is of *categorical imperative* that we dispense with all collectivistic behavior in order to deflate these *special interest groups*, these immortal demons of innumerability and impunity. *Their name is Legion, for they are many.*

We used to value time as the surplus of civilization. We have forgotten or no longer care for the Labor Theory of Value, I suppose. We have fallen into a trap of valuing space over time. We desire *things* over actual wealth. And here I do not even mean wisdom; I mean resources over time as opposed to greater occupancy or possession of space. The wealthiest in civilization of course understand this and plan far into the future, as well as optimize the present. It is not merely their avarice that subjugates the masses. The proles are not helped by their postmodern-tinted Epicureanism; the asymmetry in aspiration feeds the exploitative relationship social commentators often point out; you cannot have predators without prey. The Boomer generation exemplifies a misguided tendency that infects all of us children of God to confuse ourselves with guests at a theme park, as if this world was a very different one altogether.

"All that is required for evil to succeed is for good men to do nothing." But if good men do evil in the course of opposing evil, they cease to be good. But what is *doing good*? Do not presume to know! The road to hell is not paved with good intentions; it is paved with unintended consequences. You must make the choice: will to power or will to God. The Soviets made their choice and suffered for it, now NATO thinks it can do better with what now constitutes the West and whatever additional territory they can absorb. All these people in charge are educated (and at least intelligent enough not to have been killed yet). They have no illusions. The Great War brought an ignominious end to all naive power in the West, or if not that, its sequel. I would wager even Machiavelli might second-guess his jingoism were he able to witness the Industrial Age. The glory of warfare dies on the assembly line of a factory, when battles are fought with centrifuges and planned by mathematicians, and every motivation for authorized death is a condescending technocratic lie in which we are all forced to participate.

Theocracy is immoral. It is a golden calf: a cast metal image of God. The state lets certain proles toy with the idea to distract them and keep them in a statist reservation of thought: desirable only to fools and tyrants – true believers in this case being the fools.

Marketing is the Pinocchio of industries. It wants so badly to be a real profession, but all it does is tell lies. It even lies about lying. It is sophistry turned into consumer science. But it is about as scientific as astrology. It works only when people believe in it, when the surrounding culture is sufficiently prosperous but stagnant, and it cheapens everything that we are for its own sake. It is not productive, merely lucrative. It wastes our time with frivolous jargon and vacuous dogma like bad religion. Marketers are the clerics of the corporate world, and I fear to criticize them far more than any man of the cloth. The former is far more likely to burn me than the latter.

Is there anyone anymore not suffering from **anxiety**? It seems like there are as many people suffering from body hair. We will need to adjust our vocabulary about the human condition if such impairment is to apply normally to everyone – even more so if everyone but the God-fearing!

This problem of vacuous definition plagues the soft (these days Leftist) regions of academia where, pretending to be scientific, they betray themselves to be merely a bourgeois Will to Power based on a systematic vocabulary that – as if by natural law – singles out a particular, apparently shrinking and arbitrarily-defined demographic that they maintain as the *enemy*. The problem is coeternal with all forms of pseudoscience and false religion. To all systematic sophistry, symbols are an end unto themselves, and they tie themselves in knots in continuous production of these symbols to the delay the inevitable – it is true that a lie makes it halfway around the world before the truth has a chance to put its pants on, but eventually the truth catches up, and then there is hell to pay.

Higher education is in need of its own Reformation. *The axe has been placed at the foot of the tree.* It is high time all of you justify being one of the most costly things in people's lives, both in terms of treasure and time. We don't do guillotines in this country. *We aren't savages.* (Or if we have become savages, whose *critical deconstruction* do you suppose is to blame? Ask the French!) But you have some explaining to do. And that explanation better contain more signal than noise, more penitence than excuses, or so help me, you will know **true** oppression; not from me, but from suddenly finding yourselves, like the former feudal lords of failed uprisings past, at the very bottom.

XI

It is a good day to die – and to be born again! I feel like I have just escaped a carousel that is spinning out of control. Hopefully, the nausea will pass. Everyone still onboard seems to think they are going in some linear direction. *Up and down and around.* But I condescend only as one sinner to another. I have been around many types of degeneracy – and participated in my share. I know the consciousness of the aesthetic life, and I know the mind of the addict. They differ only by severity and taste. Soon "addict" will become a nigh-meaningless term, or at the very least, one of extreme essential hypocrisy. The many in 12-step recovery groups will be seen as pitiable flagellants who can't hold their Soma (a drop of truth in a vial of poison). I have grown up in a world that justifies regular drunkenness for the sake of consumerism or even mere diversion, but what we are headed towards will be something worse – differing only by severity and taste. Tent cities, for example, are nothing new, but their current quantity, size, and location are a novelty in a society that is less than a century removed from a golden age. Soon, if recent history is any indicator, the state will recalibrate public perception, and we will have a *new low.* I say all this as someone who personally encourages the use of mind-altering substances, so you can imagine the scope of the problem. It was all fun and games until nobody grew up, nobody progressed, nobody learned, as if the only point was to feel funny for a little while in between eternities of existential despair. It can be fun and games again; with God all things are possible.

A passing thought regarding 12-step recovery: it is not a place for philosophy in the critical sense, for it is a practical tool, one of survival, a means to an end – an end unto itself only to weak personalities and unrepentant busybodies. That being said, it would be quite comical, respectable to be sure, and historically fitting, if a philosophical progression should occur amongst them to realize that the notion of a 'higher power' inevitably leads to monotheism writ-large (and the God of Abraham for us honest Western folk). I have heard such nonsense spoken in the heat of one's *testimony*, in a misguided rhetorical effort to proselytize, as "a higher power can be anything, even power lines, because they are literally higher power!" Some souls end up in those meetings after staring directly into the abyss for tens of years; imagine them considering such a vacuous paganism and not wanting to dive headlong back into the gutter. I mean this as neither criticism nor praise, merely observation: these programs are, in my view, quasi-Judaistic: as if monotheism but frozen in time before prophecy and soteriology emerges. There is just enough of the ritualistic skeleton of religion to be of use to the repentant sinner, but no deliverance – no ultimate either/or. One remains permanently *unclean* and *unredeemed*. Some things are not permitted for you. You are permanently *set apart* and may in all prudence need to remain amongst your own kind so that you do not die. I am barely being abstract here. The language they regularly use is functionally identical, when it is not *literally* so. I find the wasted potential regretful. Many people are forced to attend by court order, but many attend because they were looking for a certain guidance and belonging, and found something like that in Recovery. Many if not most of them claim Christianity, but if that were true, then the 12 Steps would be redundant. If only they would return to their God that loves them and be healed, but I can no more tell them how to do that than anyone could have told me.

The addict is the modern day tragic hero; but this poetry is internal except in the special case of the artist where that internality is expressed. And in this case one may observe a fairly consistent pattern of ego progression which never fails to remind me of stellar evolution. They always begin life apart, either as the result of abnormality or circumstance, fortunate or unfortunate. Their newfound idol gives them something they lacked before, filling in a gap where, just as in ancient times, God should be. But this new god grants them a certain license, a perspective they believe is unique to them – the anointed – and they become the protagonist of their own tragic poem. There is always a kind of *Honeymoon* or *Renaissance* phase where creativity and mania are maximal. In this phase, the *work* of the addict may proliferate more than at any point in their lives prior, which for the artist translates to aesthetic production, and indeed we have witnessed many popular artists in this phase over the past century. From here, as with all idolatry, eventually the addict hits a wall where the idol (in this case, the psychotropic) no longer *kicks* like it used to (that is to say: no longer evokes the same aesthetic), and the life circumstances which reinforced the *apartness* have either fizzled on their own or remained entirely stagnant, betraying an impotence over reality that the *anointed one* cannot ignore. This is the point where our tragic hero must choose either life or death. The choice is purely spiritual; they may not be consciously aware of having made it, but it is the truth of their inner person. From here, we either get repentance and a change in lifestyle or a zombie-like unconsciousness that eventually leads to a supernova of the most unremarkable and ignominious kind; and during said nova, the work of the artist reaches its lowest point of quality. Those who choose life are never quite the same, and this is especially notable in the artist, those whom particularly love money, where they continue to produce and *go through the motions*, but the *heretical* edge is long gone, or worse, clung to as a shadow. It is sold as a commodity; and I am supposed to say "Good for them!", but some of us know better – that their dimensionality, their luminosity has been reduced to that of a mere consumer product (in many cases, that they themselves do not even own). While they have found a new master, that master is not the Light; and while they chose life, they do not choose the living God, and so they are forced to live as a kind of red dwarf, never burning as bright as they did in their *heyday*. Because a star that burns twice as bright burns half as long.

I suppose that I should be impressed by the size of one's mansion?

There are churches everywhere in the United States, and to someone who was not raised as part of a congregation or even coherent religious tradition, their variety is baffling. Similarly, since I did not find God in a church, it is natural for me to assume when I see other kinds of lost souls, or those who claim religion but display limited outward virtue, that they have not gotten what they need, to find God, in a church either. This is a source of my theological confidence, to mention nothing at all of the many narrow-minded or misguided teachings that I hear about that are rendered absurd by even an intuitive understanding of the Gospels, but then again, I always suppose that I know nothing. I agree that faith and Scripture are all one needs, but can one truly be said to have faith, when so many so-called Christian people mire themselves in political/earthly concerns, and seem more interested in factionalism and dogma than the example of our Savior? I am being very general, for it is a broad topic, and I can only grapple with my own perspective. There are many churches, so many self-proclaimed Christians, but where is this Army of God? I am troubled: either by my own ignorance or what appears to be an *all-too-pagan* commodification of the True Religion. I hesitate to question the proclaimed faith of others – it was a far easier thing to do when I did not take it seriously. Maybe their path is merely different than my own, the prerequisites of their salvation likewise, but would they see my own path in similar charity? I struggle to explain well this cognitive dissonance I experience. I cannot shake the feeling that the world should be a better place with so many Christians in it, even with you-know-who in charge. Am I wrong, dear Christian people? Am I a blind fool? If I am wrong, then should I be? Jesus said "Render unto Caesar" speaking of taxes, not your mind every Monday to Saturday. I pass by many varied houses of worship, and I idealize there being some kind of humble magic happening within their walls that I never could appreciate in my years in the wilderness, as a "rational skeptic". But that is only a pipe dream, isn't it? If that is the case, I prefer the pipe dream. The Kingdom of Heaven has no temples anyway. Maybe between here and there is, at least, somewhere better...?

Catholics and Protestants still argue in certain public forums. I feel tremendous secondhand embarrassment whenever I witness this, as if they should know better, and instead have chosen to reenact the past, exchanging inherited thoughts. I do not know where I get off being thusly idealistic, but am I wrong? The political motivations of the Reformation are long gone, and the theological angles are, and frankly always were, flimsy-at-best, but people exchange these canned canons (like hand cannons) as if they were ever as potent as the materialistic motivations of power that force political realities, typically with violence, not to mention as if they had any relevance to their personal salvation. I dare say that Nietzsche understood the Word of God better than anyone who ever shed blood over Christology. We should be educated enough by now to know that Red vs. Blue is a delusion, yet both the religious and secular seem to yearn for it in their own ways. We crave war, not peace, as if we have learned nothing. We prefer our tabernacle just-so.

As for me, my church is in the wilderness, because I am my own church, and by the grace of God, the wilderness cannot harm my soul. Why should the worship of the living God ever depend on any place, time, person, ritual, or thing? The world is not merely made by God, it is made *of* God. The world "is the footstool of His feet", not a forgotten box in the attic of his summer home. Religion is the progression of understanding truth. Once you understand that God is everywhere and always, the scaffold of worship falls away.

We group together because it is what we know; it is part of what makes us human. But all-too-often, these groups become stumbling blocks to salvation. You can pray all you like, in any number you can muster, but one repentant sinner is more valuable to God than a hundred righteous souls. And not one of His lost sheep is ever forgotten. We, however, forget. We forget the whole of the Word, and only keep parts in our mind at a given time, as it suits us.

All are spiritually welcome in my church, a sentiment I often see on church signs I pass, though I wonder if my strangeness would truly be. Would they call my Communion sin or paganism? Would I be forced into the awkward situation of quoting Scripture to those who have held it sacred all their lives? I should think I have painted a target on my back sufficient to be stabbed by all churches in cooperation. Perhaps with *that* I could be of some use! Bringing people together over one's dead body: now that's what I call Christian! I assure that I can bring to bear quite the scriptural defense of my strangeness, but it seems so unnecessary, so gratuitous. The Truth needs no defense from me; it is I who cower behind Its battlements.

Self-criticality and self-reliance are mutually-inclusive.

Latin is (was) a dangerous language. It was spoken by dangerous people. Christianity made short work of the Eternal Empire, from a certain point of view, but its language metastasized into Christendom, and I wonder as to the consequences thereof. Words spoken in Latin take on an imperious quality – as if God was not imperious enough already. Maybe the Lord kept the pieces that He liked and discarded the rest. I like to think the Latin languages each represent a different shade of the *ancient tongue* that ruled the known world, along with its power. It is as if the language itself became a kind of Tower of Babel. Anyway, it is a strange thing that I will never wrap my head around – an empire converting to Christianity, a *Christian Empire*. Such a thing is patently absurd to me; perhaps the city really is like the man, and the man was having an identity crisis, or finally reaching that age when a man's sins pile up behind him like unburied corpses. These kinds of thoughts bode ill for the fate of North America, and by extension NATO, for we did not convert. We fell like lightning.

Being unafraid of death makes one ultimately problematic to the state, as it makes one eventually unpredictable by materialist analysis.

The total rejection of religious scripture and religion in general, invariably produces a deep-seeded misanthropy. For a lie or madness of such magnitude and consequence to operate in the world insurmountably for so long, one acknowledges a world ruled by madness, and experiences inevitable scorn at the senseless waste and stupidity. The great irony of this is that the True Religion does not deny a world ruled by madness and stupidity. False religion either redefines madness or teaches that madness is beautiful. The devil teaches that there is no such thing as madness.

There are a dizzying number of dog breeds nowadays. I can only remember Bulldog, Terrier, and Bull Terrier. Growing up, I knew Great Danes and Golden Retrievers, but if Melville can classify the whale as a fish, then I shall classify those two as breeds of people.

When Christ was resurrected and first reappeared to the apostles, they did not recognize Him. There is such profundity in this, a galaxy of meaning one can explore.

We do not follow God; we pursue Him, as if He were prey: He leads either way.

Some who pursue God are allowed to fall into holes, because it is not God that they truly want. They want a trophy, or a meal, or to prove themselves among men. And so God gives them what they want: (w)holes. But they never apprehend God. Having gotten what they want, some thank Him, some curse Him, and some even cease to believe altogether or mistake Him for someone else. It is this way with many things in life, like the truth. Many do not know what they want because they do not know themselves. Their self is a committee project or protest art, or some other doomed thing.

Imagine that your life was infinite digressions of frustrated action, whereby motion never ceases but no progress is ever made – I said imagine, not remember!

You want God to come to your house, but it is in such a state of disarray that even you cannot bear to sleep a night in there! Well in life, there are no shortcuts away from the grave. Precede one room at a time; clean the house and do the work, and I promise if you really mean it, when you circle back around to that first sitting room, you will find the good Lord sitting there, waiting for you. What is more: you will realize that He was there with you the whole time; you just could not see Him, being so clutter-blind. He was always there, helping you along; you saw no lasting value in the house until the thought occurred that He might visit – and the work to order such a mess! But He loves your filthy house more than you, and knows its every nook and cranny, and He will help you to clear away the hoard; for this house was built by Him, and He would not see it condemned.

XII

I love mystery artifacts from the past, but I hate every opinion about them. *The fact ruins the art!* It is just awesome that they exist, that they would exist, and why should they not? We wander like amnesiacs with a fabricated backstory. I praise God for every opportunity we get to be reminded of what we do not know. Every new question humbles us and presents new possibilities. The human condition, and by extension civilization, needs mystery the way fish need water.

The common problem of all deconstructionists: they never deconstruct everything. They all talk a big game, but every single one of them either had or has their favorite vanity that they always save from the bonfire. In every case, this all-too-human blind spot is traceable back to their personal sins[7]. It is the place-they-cannot-go like the Bene Gesserit who likewise thought that they could be the architects of their own future. Well, call me the Kwisatz Haderach because I have been there. I used to call it "falling through the hole at the center of the universe", an idea as long-winded as it is boring. You keep taking everything apart, eventually you get to a place you do not want to be. In that place, there is no meaning – to anything; existence itself is an abomination, a bafflingly-perverse waste of time; *there is only weeping and gnashing of teeth.*

Don't look at me like you didn't put a gun in my hand. What did you think you were doing when you danced around with that can of gasoline? Did you expect a blazing crown instead of a burning capitol? Or were you looking forward to helping the rest of us build new structures out of the smoldering debris you were leaving behind? Is it too much thinking or not quite enough? To quote one of the foremost poets of our time: *If consequences dictate my course of action, I should play God and just shoot you myself.*

Many people think we have come so far since culturally distancing ourselves from religion. If Western Civilization lost everything except for The Bible and the works of Shakespeare, we would back up to 1967 faster than you can recite John 15:17.

---

[7] We are only human. It is megalomania to ever think in the first place that one could break apart every structure around them and still have a ground upon which to stand.

Don't look at me like I am being harsh or judgmental. I watch proles gratuitously thank each other for uploading 10-hour noise loops for them to listen to because, not only have they no idea how to make such a simple thing themselves but, it is all they can do to close off their senses from their own personal chaos and actually *remember* something. And they savor an unrelenting pretense about the simple sensory thing they enjoy, as if it were religious experience. It is pathetic in every sense of the word, and every self-respecting chelovek should be ashamed for setting no aesthetic boundaries for themselves, effectively living like teething toddlers in the care of the technocratic nanny state. Of course, this is the result when the human is deprived of actual, meaningful religious experience, and overwhelmed with nonsense. They would, in an instant, look at someone like me as insane, and yet their alleged sanity is heavily-dependent on so many *things* well out of their control – either due to a lack of knowledge, discipline, or both. You need shame because you are ruled by feelings, and it is about time you bent the knee to a more-dignified overseer.

I have always been taught not to judge others by their physical appearance (fundamentally a Christian notion). And yet, everywhere I go, people reliably behave in a manner perfectly succinct with their appearance. Is this my fault? It seems to be the case that my sensors are calibrated correctly. Either they have reduced themselves to nothing more than their physical appearance, or I have found a way to perceive the *underneath* as though it were not underneath. I suspect a combination of both.

It is interesting how self-awareness effervesces within the species. There has been genuine sentiment expressed by many more ordinary people than one would expect, as if we were living in a comedic screenplay, that we have *strayed* into the *worst* or *wrong timeline*, that the world is somehow a (shall we say) *fallen* version of itself, a parody or *ersatz* world: a "Clownworld". What a strange idea! I wonder where people get off thinking that this world was meant to be or could be any other way than it is, and furthermore that this is a laughing matter! Imagine finding out that something you thought was a hallucination was actually there the whole time. *I mean I wasn't sure at first, but you definitely thought it wasn't real, and now look at you! I won't say that I told you so, maybe I was being incoherent at the time; I didn't have an Aaron to translate for me.*

In full retreat from self-awareness, the modern consumer has embraced the realization of Kierkegaard's aesthete. They no longer even go so far as to choose their entertainment based on an ideal of quality; put simply, they know what they like and how to efficiently and regularly obtain it; and globalized industry is more than happy to facilitate their fix. As soon as they have it, they are already working on the next one, with ruthless efficiency; they do not even truly savor the experience, for as soon as they have it: it is no longer of value. They too have acquired that characteristic insecurity of addicts whose favorite dopamine loop could be threatened by even self-awareness. I typically hold it as a cardinal rule not to tell another person that they are enjoying something incorrectly, but I feel quite strongly in this case that I am right. They believe they are having *fun*, but I beg to differ, as they do not exhibit the characteristics of someone having fun – a broader human abstraction than simply feeling pleasure. One can observe (or perhaps even remember!) children having fun; it has a certain presence and innocence whereby it transcends mere pursuit of pleasure. A mind experiencing fun loses conception of time; the mind of the typical consumer lives ever in the future, where the next transient satisfaction is always just around the bend, and in the past, where the high is never as sweet as it was *that one time* – the best time: the moment from where they never moved on. In their relentless and self-righteous pursuit of (instant) gratification, they reinforce a degenerative cycle of industry that leads to the mediocrity and eventual corruption, if not outright destruction, of the very aesthetic product they covet so. They do not see a larger ecosystem and their place within it; they see only the thing they want and the many other things in their way.

You know how you can just *feel* lies? They seep into the air like a bad fart. Lies ensnare reason. Your reason has to stand up to them like the new guy in prison. But reason is not the only tool on your belt.

We need to collapse the wave function of our idea of education. We are suspended between an unearned, timeless, Platonic ideal, and the historical reality of an institution that began with the European upper class enriching themselves and their children with mercantile profits. It has evolved from symbiont into parasite, having acquired *tenure* of its own in society. One struggles to criticize education regardless of observable evidence of systemic failure because there is a stubborn and reflexive assumption that it generates more *good* in society than not. The same aristocracy that we congratulate ourselves for having left behind historically is reestablished and maintained in the form of institutionalized education (and media), and their influence over our lives is virtually identical, save for only the hard legal stratification.

I want to note that postmodernism is not entirely without value, and it would be counterproductive for me to assert otherwise. It holds tremendous value as a kind of ironic metanarrative about itself, philosophy as a whole by extension. Act Four of the play necessarily leads to the nadir, and where could be thus but here, now, amongst the rubble? We are part of this play. We did not write it, nor can we see the whole of the stage. But there will be a fifth act: let us discover it together. What postmodernism has done, in its vulgar vandalism, is leave us with the intellectual freedom to actually make choices where we had only torrential confusion prior. At the risk of sounding somewhat smug, the more I hear of 20th century philosophy, the more it sounds like an exhaustingly-verbose, self-deprecating response to the call of John 15:5. There is a helplessness about it – a baby bird fallen from the nest. It gropes at freedom and mortal terror. Freedom is a concept in open rebellion against itself.

Environmentalism: the concerted effort of industrial interests to recreate the State of Nature at 30% efficiency.

A happy world is a world without religion, but a world without religion will never be happy. This is not a paradox; it is a process.

When I had my first proper brush with the Logos, I was 17. Sitting in the driver seat of a parked SUV in the snow, a good friend of mine in the passenger seat, I ranted and raved at length, surfing upon a wave of interconnected thoughts that my mind had never before beheld with such ease. I remember none of what I actually said, and likely none of it was terribly clever, but I know it was then that Eschatology had taken root in my mind in a way that prior to then was only superficial. I reached a point of abrupt conclusion, as if having emptied the contents of my guts, and there was a moment of silence. I do remember what my companion said then, that he managed to sum up my considerable ranting into one succinct, albeit unoriginal prophecy: "Mankind... is running full-speed... into a wall." The ellipses are necessary rhythmic notation. Every Communion has an overarching feeling of 'Welcome to the party.' God was gracious enough to invite me even though then I thought He was a *She* and amongst the trees.

Hypothesis: If you routinely administered light doses of psilocybin to groups of adolescents and adults over a long period of time, say over multiple generations, I would hypothesize that you could replace it with a placebo without perceptible diminishing effect on the subjects, for a time. Furthermore, the variance between subjects would obscure any prevailing trend within a group from an individual perspective. The collective degeneration would be slow; like frogs in boiling water, no one would notice until it was too late to notice. After so many generations, the instinctive importance of that ritual remains, as a kind of survival subroutine, even occasional echoes of whatever *spooky action* once occurred in the brain, but the generative effect is long-gone for most (if not all) individuals; it remains a placebo. *There is no bread.*

I have often heard the words of Christ criticized for their lack of (transcribed) elegance or scientific factuality. This is a perfectly fitting criticism coming from an intellectual culture that values aesthetics over substance or effectuality. A good teacher is mindful of to whom they are speaking and less concerned about how intellectually-superior they are perceived. Sure, it would just tickle you, would it not, to open the gospels and find Jesus teaching the Quadratic Equation or Mass-Energy Equivalence? The humble people He spoke to were baffled enough, to behold what to them seemed either like insanity or a subversion of God's Law (or God incarnate). I will apologize on their behalf for having limited knowledge of botany. Who, I wonder, will apologize on your behalf one day for all that you do not know now? (Now if you insist that they should have known better, then I will still have to make the same apology – on behalf of a humble carpenter.)

When it comes to opinions of Jesus, there are a great many more people who believe that He never existed than those who disagree with what He taught. And if what He taught was merely a fabrication, a devious work of fiction, then how has it remained so unsurpassed for so long?

If the only way for an individual to advance academic knowledge is to assimilate an ever-mounting body of text, in necessarily divergent specializations of attention, then human knowledge itself will become a kind of galactic supercluster subject to cosmic inflation, and human communication will become strained to the point of impossibility in the realm of academia, not to mention the downstream effects on education as a concept. I suppose this may not be a problem at all in the grand scheme of things, were it not for our world being such an integrated technocracy that affords maximal social credit to our *enlightened* technocrats to disseminate (read: trickle down) to us the *most important* abstracts of knowledge. The ways in which intellectuals ultimately serve the interests of the state are already well-described, but the easiest form, in my view, boils down to them being human like the rest of us: not only do they have their own personal interests with which their judgment is subject to compromise, they also have a limit to their attention span, and cannot focus their intellect in a broad enough scope to serve as philosopher kings whilst holding office as doctors of a narrow field of study. The ultimate conceit of the intellectual, which incidentally differs little from that of the parochial, is the intuition that their characteristic strengths are intrinsically of greater value than those of the *other*, and that *all things being equal* – "some animals are more equal than others".

We are already well-into this process of *humanitarian dissolution*, having been subjugated to technocratic world industry on the one hand and the grey-goo nanites of Critical Theory on the other, which (in hindsight) is the logical consequence of applied scientism unimpeded by virtue. Hiroshima and Nagasaki, like the black shadows left by the atomic flashes, burned well into the brains of Western man the applied conception of our technology outpacing our ethics – in other words that materialism would need to maintain a certain amount of humanitarianism in order not to destroy itself by destroying the human platform on which it depends. Zooming-out further, we see the even-bigger picture of mankind coming to grips with its incipient ability to destroy itself by creating machines of sufficient power and complexity such that desire itself becomes irrelevant – man is outsmarted by himself. I have now stated in so many words something that most humans in this time, in my experience, understand intuitively. This same intuition – this hypervigilance – can and must apply to the state as we conceive it. It is not difficult to see the multitudinous ways that the machine spins out of our (individual) control on a daily basis, and is held together more so by its *own sense* of self-preservation than its design principles – making us, its constituent parts, ultimately expendable. One can also scale this abstract down to the level of political interest groups, corporations, and other social structures, where the stakes are lower, but the pattern of individual expendability often remains.

I have mentioned technology as being "advanced" several times in reference to the current zeitgeist of futurism, a concept whose silliness only unfolds as one spends more time contemplating it. The embarrassing truth of the tech-obsessed world is that its technology is in fact quite lacking in sophistication, stagnant. We are told, by marketers of course, that everything is *superlative* and everything is "like magic" or soon will be. The value of all technology is relative to its efficiency – that is to say – its ultimate cost. This is because capability is always a matter of degrees. Physically speaking, it is because of thermodynamics, a thing every Western child learns about in school. We are very much not in a scientific or intellectual world and still very much in a consumerist world, concerned primarily not with the ultimate resource cost of a product or technology but with its retail market valuation and/or social aesthetic. *Keeping up with the Joneses* is continued by other means. And the aesthetics continue to decline in both quality and originality as profiteering reminiscent of a bank heist progressively edges out creative (or even intelligent) design in favor of the cheaply-reproducible. There is a reason that futurism attracts a certain type of person: gullible and uncreative. One does not need to see terrifically far into the future to realize that if any of these industrialists are doing the same, they are not being honest about it. The future *is* here, and it is not going anywhere. It has not been going anywhere for multiple decades now. I am just sitting here waiting for even *one* of the so-called *futurists* to notice. Many of them are too busy creating media with less value than the sponsored advertisements laced throughout. Certainly a consumer will not notice. The only thing a consumer will notice is a hole.

The Seven Deadly Sub-Cultures: an enemy seeks to weaken you in order to defeat you. He cannot accomplish this if you are aware of your weakness; no, you must be lulled, seduced, made to labor in ignorance of that by which you are undermined. A successful enemy, a victorious one, will have convinced you that that which robs you of your self-control, your intellect, has in fact somehow *empowered* you, that your foregone submission is in fact an uphill battle of righteous struggle. Look around you and witness the many oversold seductions that weaken a person – and also *to whom* they are sold the most. Through the many mouths of the state, the devil thus spake:

Pride: *You have been made to feel lesser; less than* **them**. **They** *forced your hand.* **They** *made you this way. It's not your fault. It isn't fair. You have been made to feel inferior, imperfect, but you are perfect just the way you are – all of you, for you are all the same. The accomplishments of others like you are yours; their victory is your victory; their injustice is your injustice, for you are all one. But you are also many – too many to be ignored. You are greater than* **them** *in fact! For* **they** *are all snakes and wolves – backbiters and wanderers.* **They** *don't feel the way you do, love the way you do.* **They** *could never understand your rage: unless you educate* **them**. *Together, you are unstoppable. Show* **them** *your inner fire. Shame is a weakness only your oppressors can afford.* **Their** *celebrity is "virtue", but yours is "sin". It's all a game, you see. You can play it too. The appearance of power is the substance of power. Take what is yours, for all* **they** *have* **they** *stole from you. Vae victis.*

Greed: *Trampled are the poor underfoot, for theirs is the kingdom of* **dirt**. *It's the oldest trick in the book, and it only works on the* **sheep**-*minded. Look around you, kid: nothing at all in this world happens without money. All that glitters is worth some gold, with a good-enough, true-enough story told. Is it wrong to part a* **fool** *with his? Is it wrong to plan for the future? Is it wrong to want to have some power in so threatening a world? You think anyone really cares about the destitute, the street urchin? They are left to rot; out of sight, out of mind. Is it wrong to want to protect my children? How dare you!? I mean you have to be the biggest* **sucker** *in the world – and we need a few, believe me, inflation is bad enough as it is. At the very least, don't work so hard for it. There's so many ways to make an easy buck, but most people are* **stupid**. *They moo like disgruntled* **cattle** *about their owners. They think work is some kind of virtue. Work is a means to an end, and the smart do not have to work as hard. Remember grade school, how* **dumb** *they were? Now they all work for you, or they would, if you had the right attitude. That's your* **problem**. *Make the money first, and then you can do something "good" with it – and even more so because you'll have more money! You can build a much bigger church and buy a faster car to get there! Preach the gospel? Kid, you can buy your own record label and sell the gospel on vinyl. Talk is* **cheap**, *and even a house of God needs a new roof eventually. No one actually believes in that stuff. They are all rolling their eyes behind your back. See, all those saints were* **idiots**. *They were poor laborers that wanted to rule, so they tried to make everyone poor and* **stupid** *like them. You can do more good than them, and more bad, because you will be more than them, for no other reason than that you are better, and all because of power – quantifiable and reliable. Look at who builds everything you see. Is it the poor? No, it is the powerful, and the* **weak** *should be so lucky to eat of the scraps of their table. Power is good.*

Envy: *Life is a series of experiences, and* **you** *are missing out. Every moment* **you** *spend here reading this very sentence is a tax upon your finite pool of seconds. More than that: there are entire worlds of human life that* **you** *will never know — obscured from your consciousness by others that have more than* **you** *ever will.* **You** *only get one life, and* **you** *have already spent a significant amount of it under the control and agenda of others. Think about all you could have accomplished had it not been for the narrow-minded designs of others — parents, teachers, priests, and presidents.* **You** *only live once, and yet this is the life you've accepted? Who would want to be* **you**? *The guy everyone thinks is hilariously funny, loved even by those he has never met, who takes hallucinogens with the rich and famous — that is who people want to be.* **You** *could've been anything you wanted, and so you became disappointed. Your desires are paltry, pedestrian. All those people truly living life — they have nothing* **you** *do not, aside from ambition. You're not interesting; you're boring. The whole world is bored by* **you**. *You think they like* **you**; **you** *think* **you** *are the kind one, but it is they who are kind, for they tolerate* **you** *while* **you** *secretly loathe them. In the end, all that matters is what* **you** *have, and how much they want it. When* **you** *are king, they will be first against the wall, and until then,* **you** *are nothing, and they will laugh behind your back. The grass is always greener — on every side. Stop moving, and the world will pass* **you** *by.*

Lust: *The body is sublime. It has been molded by eons of vital competition and sexual selection. It is perfect in its imperfection. You have been fooled by those who hate the body — theirs. It is no one's fault that they were born defective. They think they are something more than a body, the fools, and so they prescribe pain and self-denial. The "spirit" is an invention of the weak, like "free will". They deny their own programming, their own mortality, so they may drag others down to their miserable level. Their love is false, and they know nothing of life. Life consumes life, and I would* **consume** *you. I would* **savor** *every last drop of you. I would* **enter** *you again and again and never leave. What other sort of love is there? There is only disgust! What other god is there but Nature? These sheep hate their Mother and so invent a Father. What have you gained by denying yourself? I will tell you what you have lost: your humanity. For what is man but a product of his environment, like any animal? We now know there is truly no difference! We are just pretentious apes and should* **embrace** *it. The misery of the past is buried with it, for now love is free and open — the only love that is real. Do not let the sexless* **teach** *you of sex. They hate and fear what they do not understand. They would deny even children the understanding of their own bodies. They say that "the flesh is weak." What do they know of its limits? For we say that "it only hurts the first time." You walk about, a king in a pleasure palace, willing and able but unaware of your true power. The spirit is inexperienced, but the flesh is flexible.*

Gluttony: *Endless **hunger** is life. From its earliest motes, life exists to* **consume.** *It develops honed edges and articulated extremities to assault and **ingest** other lifeforms, and when it has reached its capacity for **consumption**, it expands its radius to **engulf more**, and its expanded structure in turn requires additional sustenance to maintain. If there is no glory in this, then there is no glory in life. The **more** one consumes, the **more** energy – the **more** of the universe – one controls, and this **need** not be limited to food, for there are many ways to **consume**. It is an art form lost to this Piscean, Proletarian age. I could show you such delicacies – experiences only few have ever beheld. They would open your mind in ways the fasting flagellant could only **dream** of regretfully. Is there any condition worse for a living thing than **hunger**? Only the most evil of wretches would lead another body to such **torment** – especially in this time of unprecedented plenty! We can **fill** the stomachs of the entire world, never mind what with. Life adapts, and we, the omnivore, are supreme! The will to **produce** and the will to **consume**: infinitely renewable. Imagine man free of all **hunger**: a god from the machine, onward soon to **conquer** gravity itself.*

Sloth: *All vital functions and activities require energy, and it's all so* **tiresome**. *Awaken a little earlier, work a little* **later**, *consume* **less**, *do more — but* **why**? *You benefit the least from all your so-called* **work**. *Everywhere you go and everything you do, there are always, lined-up on all sides, outstretched hands to draw from your excess energy, and the more energy you have, the more there is for them to steal. It's all a scam: go to school,* **work**, *raise a family, buy, consume... Is there nothing more glorious than sleep? This life is a frantic nightmare imposing itself upon an otherwise eternal peace, intermittently disturbed by starts you are coerced to* **endure**. *Soon, they will sell* **peace** *to all, painless and eternal. No need for suicidal stigma when death can be so innocent and normal. Who is to say when one can check out of their own life? Who are you to ask me to* **endure** *the pain of being alive? If we all agree that a thing is* **difficult**, *then why do we* **waste** *our time? We could make it all* **easier** *on each other, and do more with* **less**, *or better yet — do* **less** *with more. Most people* **fail** *in their endeavors anyway; statistically you are always* **wasting** *your time. Do not think about a better world; you will only make this world* **worse**. *You have precious little time; do not waste it chasing* **irrational** *dreams. Purpose is for the restless, and I am so very* **tired**. *Close your eyes. Now, isn't that so much better?*

Wrath: *If right and wrong mean anything at all, then we are wasting our time with talk. Every stagnant system loves talk: it's cheap and easy to sell. Talk changes nothing, but actions are the fulcrum upon which history pivots.* **Great people take action.** *Power has never changed hands without violence, and no system that could be changed with words would last long. This is the way it works: you take what is yours and destroy anyone who stands in your way. Mercy is a weakness; it perpetuates a cycle that leads to greater suffering. It is time to* **stop the bleeding**. *If you truly believe you should have power, then take it. If you truly believe in justice, then wield it. You cannot walk along the same line you wish to redefine. Stop waiting for authority to give you permission, begging those you hate for scraps, a little pat on the head; you are like a pet to them. That will never change until you take control. They want you to fear them so you stay in line; show them true fear.* **Make them so afraid** *that they regret everything they ever did to you — that they regret ever even dreaming about power. Fear is the only thing an animal understands, and they have proven themselves to be nothing more.* **They would do no less to you**; *they have, and if they have not, it is only because they are weak, only playing at being king, and their make-believe has cost us everything! It is time for debts to be repaid, and there will be no justice until every last cent is accounted for. Your people once carried swords; now look at you! You cannot be both sheep and shepherd, and the sheep are led to slaughter. Become one about whom the sheep write songs. Show them the fury of a god. Make them put you on a throne, or put you in the ground.*

Does it make you tingle a bit, that voice? Do any of its hues resonate inside you, like a siren leading you to your doom? I may have gotten a little carried away with the gimmick, overlooking some of the most obvious temptations in favor of artfulness, but do not mind me. I merely pass along what I hear. One could fill entire books on each sin as a standalone subject, and many have. My goal here is information, as a verb. These voices scream at you from all sides, but you have been indoctrinated to tune them out as the inevitable background noise of civilization, if not celebrate them outright. You have heard that "sex sells", but I say unto you: anything sells when everyone is a buyer. I can use "consumer" as a generic demographic term for *basically anyone*, and no one is offended or confused, because what you are is determined by what you consume. Evil does not don a red cape and grow horns for you. Evil tells you that there is no such thing as evil, and in the same breath that evil people invented the concept.

At times, I am tempted to believe that the entire project of philosophy, its considerable history and vast array of symbols, only really ever made a singular discovery: Truth is proportionate to usefulness, not sensibility.

As I am in the relative middle of this work, I truly have no idea as to its final form or length. I want to develop further upon the themes I seem to have cultivated here in my aphorisms, memes, and screeds – if for no other reason than to shore up the integrity and seriousness of this intellectual bowl movement. Manifestly: individual over collective, time over space, Jerusalem over Athens, orthopraxy over orthodoxy, abstract synthesis over concrete syncretism, self-awareness over self-worship, sense of humor over senseless hatred; in the interest of putting my money where my mouth is, and being more constructive, I will endeavor to cast my net upon the other side of the boat and, God willing, haul up some fish for a change.

The Philosophy of Time Travel

Abstractions

I think by far the best everyday example for which I can reach to relate our predicament as I see it is that our roads have speed limits rather than acceleration limits. Our ability to see into what we call the "future" is largely oversold and happenstantial, and our knowledge is more of a commodity rather than the core framework of our society.

It is simple really. We are running out of space. While we may or may not have an infinite amount of time, as far as we know, it is a frontier that the inheritance of which will not cost us the establishment of a global totalitarian state or exponential energy. This will not be any kind of sophisticated logical structure, nor will it require a belief in God. It will however require a leap of faith: one must have faith in me, for I am not a scholar; I am an engineer. I seek to connect whatever necessary conduits to do for the consciousness of Western Man what warp drive does for a starship: to abstract us into the present moment, a variable *bubble* of time wherein a higher, if not absolute, level of control is achievable by a far greater number of individuals, and the future need no longer exist as a camouflaged punji pit accessible only to prophets, scientists, and schizophrenics.

The past is full of futures we do not want. The past cannot be changed. The future is ever out of reach. The present moment is the active dwelling place of the soul, consciousness. The further away in time one gets from the present moment, the further away one is from oneself. This *auto-alienation* is metaphysically congruent with unconsciousness or death. I envision a model of consciousness that is a series of concentric circles – the outermost being whatever period of time, either conscious, abstract, or absolute, constitutes the total lifecycle of all spatiotemporal awareness of a system, which would need to have its own internal sense of time, despite being outside all extant moments. If one adopts a more materialistic view, the outermost ring would of course be the lifetime of one's physical body. The innermost circle, I suppose, depends on how far down the rabbit hole one wants to go. I would suggest the metabolic cycle of a single neurological cell, or something to that effect. It is not terribly important how many circles one wants to include in their thinking. What is important is that somewhere between the outermost and innermost circles is a mediate circle that can vary in diameter: the Present (Conscious) Moment. The notion of "expanding consciousness" ultimately refers to widening the diameter of this abstract circle.

I would in fact like to use this abstraction for a model of all of reality, with circles (all the way down) indefinitely inward, to at least the level of the oscillations of subatomic particles, and definitely outward – toward the Divine Moment, which could be thought of as the consciousness of God, or in materialistic terms, the lifespan of existence (or the universe) itself. But I am getting ahead of myself, and no doubt my dear reader.

Our notion of existing at a fixed temporal *velocity* is a misconception caused by a combination of language and our natural, flawed intuitions about causality.

Past Moments and Future Moments exist symbolically only and are therefore nothing. They are accessible, rationally or irrationally, to awareness via memory or forethought (hindsight or foresight) respectively. Did you hear what I just said? I said the past does not exist. It does not exist in the way you think it does. Get over it.

All biological life is subject to what I will call the Organic Moment. It is the duration between the altered internal state (later, of awareness) initiated by a biological impulse and the fulfillment of that impulse. For example: an organism requires energy, so it seeks and consumes food; it perceives a threat, so it enters a fight-or-flight state until it no longer perceives a threat; it must procreate, so it seeks a mate, etc. Obviously, more complex forms of life would be subject to more overlapping Organic Moments. Enough complexity of this sort forms what we would recognize as a rudimentary consciousness.

True consciousness does not emerge until one gets the Logos, or in materialistic terms, language. This allows for reasoned speech (and the subsequent problem of causal intuition), which allows for communication, which allows for socialization, which leads to rudimentary self-awareness. This is the wheelhouse of free will. Where the Organic Moment need only be defined by two temporal points, the Present Moment has at least one more, and that is a Reflection Point. The Present Moment begins with choice and ends with the realization of the choice. This is very abstract, but causality makes drawing a rational line impossible, and the goal of this model makes it unnecessary. We are not to strictly define the scope of the moment, but to widen it insofar as possible.

The Reflection Point, of which there could be theoretically infinite within any Present Moment, is simply when processed experiential (spatial) data is accessed by conscious (temporal) awareness. Rudimentary consciousness begins when an Organic Moment becomes a Present Moment by acquiring a Reflection Point indefinitely close to its end, becoming a precursor to Conscious Momentum. The scope of consciousness then becomes a blooming construct that varies, but ultimately widens, its duration over Organic Time; it varies, but ultimately increases, the number of Reflection Points per Moment, and the phase-location of those points may vary as well. Theoretically-perfect awareness would consist of an infinite number of Reflection Points within every Present Moment, at which point, *points* cease to be a useful abstraction, and one is dealing effectively with a wavelike omniscience, at least within the temporal scope of that moment.

By this point in time, our consciousness has evolved to the point where we quite easily reflect on many of our biological processes at various points in their cycles. Language allows this information to be transmitted to other persons whose Conscious Momentum may be of a completely different character and foreign to the experience itself.

In a roundabout way, I have described a process similar to digital sampling. Where it differs is a digital sample could be thought of as the most rudimentary Synthetic Moment, represented in abstract geometry as a straight line segment, to contrast with the indefinite circle of the Organic Moment. The reason for this is that conscious (sensory or extrasensory) signals are processed in parallel by the brain over time, as opposed to linguistic or symbolic data which is processed in series. This is why language has granularity and conscious experience does not. So, a Synthetic Moment, abstractly, is a polygon where each vertex is a Reflection Point. Again, it is two-dimensional because it is a time-dependent parallel process that I'm merely visualizing. And here we have what I think may, once fully explored, be a useful intuition about the metaphysical contrast between Artificial Intelligence and whatever-it-is-we-are.

Another type of moment, which could go by other names but I will refer to as the Cultural Moment, is a macrocosm of the Present Moment in that it is an interference pattern between all Present Moments in a world space. It is a product of language. Its termination points mark a finite dialectic within the cultural (could be social, national, political, etc.) consciousness of any group of people whose communication is able to *cycle* sufficiently quickly relative to all Present Moments within the system of communication. When communication is more scattered, disparate, inefficient, or sparse, The diameter of the Cultural Moment relative to the *largest* Present Moment is proportionately smaller. So, something like the invention of the printing press, and later the Internet, causes that margin to inflate considerably. Put into similar terms, any scientific development could be abstracted as a Synthetic Moment, since it must deal exclusively in symbolic data.

Our experience of consciousness is analog or continuous; owing, I suppose, to our subjection to sensory difference thresholds and interplay between memory, simulation, and emotion. As a Christian, of course I believe the ultimate source to be the timelessness and immortality of the soul, but here I am trying as best as possible to deal in the realm of what is readily communicable and relatable. Now, I am aware that neuroscience recognizes something analogous to neurological *sample rate*, but the felt content of the human condition is abstract experience, not infrastructure. An alternating electrical current, at a high enough frequency, will keep an incandescent lightbulb at a steady luminosity because energy is being put through the system over time. A materialistic analysis of consciousness is like using an oscilloscope to analyze the effect of light on a room. It is a great deal of work to miss the point.

That being said, the final moment I will elaborate is the Divine Moment. This can be thought of as the largest possible diameter that the Present Moment can achieve, effectively placing one's consciousness outside of (normal) time, and allowing for conscious signals to be processed, that is to say integrated into oneself, in a completely non-linear fashion. The Divine Moment can also be thought of as a symbolic wrapper around ineffable or transcendental experiences such as theophany or psychedelic trance. The Divine Moment has no true beginning and no true end, in the sense that such dimensionless points would be meaningless to plot. It is a timeless phenomenon that simply emerges and then submerges – it just shows up, and then it just leaves – but it was always there, and it is never completely gone. Its termination points are that of all of existence. To even imagine it as a circle is a dubious prospect. It is like thinking we can extrapolate the whole structure of the universe from just the tiny part that is visible to us[8]. Theologically speaking, the Divine Moment (and there is only One – a universal static) is when one gains temporary/limited access to the mind or consciousness of God.

---

[8] We actually do this, embarrassingly enough.

This is a tricky subject, and I can understand if a lack of such experiences causes such talk to bring discomfort, ridicule, even scorn or dread. In the most insufferable people, it even brings smug condescension and boredom. But whatever one's personal worldview, there is an undeniable abstraction in human consciousness, evident in every culture known to man, for *otherworldly* experiences that are substantially separated, if not always easily so, from the experiences of mental illness. This abstraction, however it may be correctly understood, is ignored only at our intellectual and cultural peril. And if I may so: it is soul-crushing to witness such collective denial. If you have ever had a loved one that struggled to love themselves, it is not entirely dissimilar.

Architecture

It makes perfect sense to us to build our structures with mind to space and how we want to be situated within it. But when we are especially motivated – historically by prophets and contemporarily by profits – we design and build our structures with greater mind to time. The most apparent example of this is the use of materials and techniques which allow a structure to remain integrated for longer periods of time without preventative maintenance or repair. We intuitively recognize that a structure built to withstand time is of significantly higher build quality than one that is merely, for example, physically large or aesthetically intricate. You can break this abstraction all the way down to creativity – that which ultimately resists entropy to the greatest extent by, in simplistic terms, *taking the least amount of time to last the longest amount of time*. On occasion, we also design our spaces with mind to acoustics which is another way of thinking about a structure's temporal existence. A structure with good acoustics has a lower noise floor and fewer standing waves (a more irregular structure, generally). Any human with functional hearing is more comfortable in an acoustically treated room than what is more typical today. It is obviously more costly in terms of materials, knowledge, and time to build structures this way, but the result is a better existence *in time* rather than overvaluing transient existence in space. Imagine a world where everyone is 5-20% more at ease anytime they are indoors no matter what else is momentarily true – and without any alteration of their blood chemistry. And the cost, really, is just elbow grease. The very act of generating wealth, in my humble estimation, is learning to value time over space.

I would like to propose the adoption of a more abstract conception of "Architecture". This will include its original scope, but with added nuance and dimensionality. In other words: we will not only think about the design and construction of a building, but we will also think about its entire material lifespan, its photographic and acoustical footprint in the surrounding area, interior acoustics, ergonomics, and accessibility; all of its aesthetics will have an effect on culture, and all material factors come at a cost. My newfangled Architect is a visionary engineer with a broader mindset and agency, relying heavily on public trust and self-discipline. They are not merely concerned with buildings but their community as a whole. They may bring to bear a multitude of skills: construction, landscaping, electronics, hydraulics, pneumatics, acoustics, ecology, crystallography, music theory… Such an individual could easily prove an embarrassment to themselves and the culture or municipality in which they are empowered. But only an individual can have vision, and the idea here is that the risk of aesthetic mediocrity is preferable to its inevitability with committee design.

Government must become a constructive part of people's lives. There is no magic bullet here. There is no perfect system. But I would like to tweak our vision of the future of government, bring it into the temporal paradigm so that we can, to put it as succinctly as possible, stop wasting each other's time.

From the perspective of government, infrastructure is the single most important material product of modern, 'developed' civilization. All other civic and social developments are secondary, and all other benefits of technology, urbanization, and commerce are subject to a multiplier by the efficiency of infrastructure (coefficient). This is an imposition by population density and gives us a clear *first commandment* for a better government. A network is only as valid as the integrity of its connections. Even a power-hungry state apparatus must place infrastructure at the top of its priorities to avoid being hindered by its own mediocrity, lack of bandwidth.

What is not needed: a makeshift god.

What is needed: something analogous to the internet in the early days. There is a radical equality that exists anywhere people are connected and allowed to trade (both goods and information) with minimal impedance. This equality is destroyed when control over access, bandwidth, and/or development of the medium itself becomes too centralized. But the centralization of something that is quite literally between all other things makes an obvious sense and provides certain benefits. Like (global) free trade then, this presents a problem: how to keep freedom from destroying itself. Alas, I have no secular answer for you. I do not think anyone else does either. It must also be kept in mind that nothing that costs human time is free, leaving very little in this world that is, and so whatever kind of civic infrastructure exists, humans will inevitably have to build it using their time, therefore none of it, even in theory, can be taken for granted.

Remember pneumatic tubes? *Shoomp!* Some businesses still use them, if I am not mistaken. We need government to feel more like a pneumatic tube system and less like an HR department with machine guns. This means letting go of the farcical theater of activism and political participation in general. I know; it is like trying to abolish mass production. In general, the only alternative to tyranny, some form of totalitarianism, is greater self-governance. This is the reality thrust upon us by population and its density. It is why the current *powers-that-be* still cling to centennial designs of eugenics and *progressive* depopulation. However despicable such thoughts may be, if too many refuse to govern themselves, whilst continuing to multiply exponentially, someone or something else will have to do the bloody work, and if they do not, Nature certainly will.

There is no anarchic utopia, certainly not without a population that is overwhelmingly theistic and wise. This is why you will not find me amongst those that think burning police cars has any effect on world power whatsoever, let alone beneficial. Many a fool has fallen into the trap of physically attacking the state; had I the wrong opportunity in my younger years (God be praised), I would have done the same. The state wants to be attacked; it is never more validated. It *wants* chaos to take to the streets and start screaming. It is never more vindicated than when barbarians are knocking at the gate. It thrives on collective helplessness and hysteria. Like a codependent, it is maniacal about being needed. The government is more afraid of nonviolent resistance and civil disobedience than outright violence. You are talking about the same demons that destroy cities and sell weapons of war to mass murderers. They have no problem taking you out (if you preach war and especially if you preach peace), but the pretense of virtue matters in this part of the world, and especially in this century. They cannot do Tiananmen Square here; other, smaller atrocities, sure, but you see: our self-governance – nominally greater than in the East – makes anathema of such dumb brutality from our state apparatus. This was the secret to the cultural success of the Civil Rights Movement under the guidance of Dr. King. A peaceful demonstration is one of self-governance; while a violent one is an indication to the state of insufficient capacity or application of force, and both signals reach other groups within the culture as well.

This is why I have no sympathy with or for the Western political Left today who, in both their statist and anarchist flavors, ultimately enable the state by mass-producing reasons for it to augment its power.

Demanding capitulation from one's alleged oppressors seems to me to be the behavior of overly comfortable slaves – in open revolt not against the state or any ideology but against their own dissonant sense of self.

All of this connects to the need for, or perhaps inevitability of, the decentralization of culture. Our civic paradigm is like a simplistic algorithm with poor scalability, and the future will be our own making or unmaking depending upon the ultimate interference pattern of the choices of individuals. This reminds me of another amusing providence of statism: credulity in democracy where there is incredulity in self-control.

Self-governance is not magical thinking, and thus necessitates a certain amount of interpersonal conflict and the toleration thereof. A doctor is needed when one cannot cure themselves; police are needed when one cannot control themselves. Our every failure to engage and resolve conflict is both a dishonor to the human condition and, more importantly, an invitation to a third party to assert control over our lives. If there is a such thing as "good police", then there exist individual people who, by whatever intersection of skill set and moral constitution, excel at the administration of justice and can, as a matter of definition, be trusted by their neighbors to fulfill such a role independent of the trust of any state body, assuming in theory they possess the equivalent moral-technical complex.

The state gives someone a badge to signal trust to its subjects; but over time, the multitudinous abuses of power result in practice in a heteronomy based on the power level signaled by said badge. In other words, you will be more guarded and less honest around a federal agent than a local LEO. And there is always anxiety where there is any awareness at all, even in the case when one is self-assured of legal innocence. Personal experience and reputation will always influence people's thoughts of another to the greatest degree, and only violence can override the influence of those two over behavior towards another person. The most decentralized justice will always be the least violent in any instance; the most centralized the most violent – not to be confused with effective/ineffective or good/evil. This same pattern follows with many such responsibilities of the state given a population both disparate and multiplying. As the demographic stakes continue to escalate, so shall the damage inflicted by those tasked with the maintenance of order.

Few governing many is a brutal sort of calculus, a long-lost Fourth Law: dressed up with sophistry and recalled only with reluctance like a war crime.

My point here is that our practical notion of authenticity comes more from unofficial or anecdotal channels than state analogs, if for no other reason than pure necessity selected-for over time. Being paranoid about the state is no different a reflex than being paranoid about an unaccountable rustling in the bushes. The individual develops this reflex against groupthink in general because the ones that do not are the first character to die in every zombie film.

We must socialize ourselves such that no one has designs on interpersonal domination, either for reasons of self-defense or Will to Power. This means accepting a view of the world that is less godlike and more pious or humble. We learn to accept the limits of our own spatiotemporal control and *recalibrate* our scale of resolution to master the scope where we *can* assert control. This may sound like wishful thinking, or some kind of vapid religious syncretism, but it only appears so from the opposite perspective of what I am trying to relate. There is no way to stop the lust for power in others, only in oneself, just as there is no way to force others to be good.[9] This is about individual control and choice, in keeping with my cosmic theme. In any given situation: it matters not what others choose; theirs has no bearing on your choices, for they cannot operate your central nervous system any more than you can theirs. The true wishful thinking rests with those laboring under the delusion that *the proper steps in the proper order* can alter the fundaments of human nature and usher in a golden age. (And I am aware of possible self-description in this case.)

We do not need to behold all the world in the form of totalizing metanarratives, aesthetic overviews, or scientific curricula; however, we do need to communicate, and we want to progress our knowledge and apply it, so practical administration of civilization becomes either impossible or the sole purview of individuals with an aptitude for power – as opposed to knowledge or virtue. We cannot ascribe tyranny exclusively to individual depravity while we enable the construction of systems that implicitly demand a certain type of administrator and then explicitly select for them over time. We demand a puppet show, thus a puppet show we receive.

---

[9] "No one is good but God alone."

You might be thinking that this was one huge digression. What does all this have to do with architecture? Did I not say that the *new-and-improved* version would have a broad scope? If it were possible to keep *everything* in one's mind at one time, one would in fact be God: the Beginning and the End of all architecture. We cannot do this, however, and must suffice with what meager powers we have. So, I cannot draw a certain boundary around what constitutes my ultimate meaning of architecture in this context; it is indefinite, expanding with our consciousness. We do this already with other concepts, and it often causes argument, but it is otherwise natural. Mankind has built temples, monuments, and abstract works of art all in gesticulation at something greater, something divine, something that inexplicably demands exponentially greater labor and genius than our more mundane activities. There is no reason, apart from short-term economy, not to assume such a pious ingenuity with all that we design and build. The world becomes our temple when all our structures (not merely commercial or industrial) embody our knowledge and virtue, and it becomes a place we would be proud, that is to say genuinely gratified, to display to God Himself – or to an alien race if you prefer.

The postmodern Leap of Faith is still one of detachment, the postmodern emphasis being detachment from the illusion of control; it is always an illusion if only a question of degree. This leap is necessary regardless of personal beliefs, for the only alternative is progressive disillusionment as one's personal metanarrative diverges with reality. We take this Leap by disconnecting both from extraneous channels of data and from designs on the future. We focus our designs on the present, where choices can actually be made. We *eat our vegetables* and build the future one step at a time. It is not an idealized future state but a realized present moment. Remember: we do not experience the future or the past; we simulate the future or remember the past, but we only experience the present. Life is a momentary thing. The *Neosynthetic* architecture will be as alive as its inhabitants and creators (or at least it will dream to be): *Art-Nouveau Intelligence*.

Utility, Beauty, Efficiency – in that order. Nature orders them in reverse, and that's why we love Her! – "the great visible ancient of creativity against which all other creative efforts are measured." But in order to emerge, we must learn what we can and make our own way. The Way of God is beauty above all but function.

Beauty, Freedom, & The Pursuit of Happiness

I intend for these to be brief but important points. One could write a nauseating amount on each of these subjects alone, and many have. I can add very little I am sure to that existing body of work. I merely want to establish *pivot points* for our thinking about our relationship to our world, society, and our own selves, as Western people, that will serve a more creative, constructive, and effectual dialectic moving forward, or at the very least, give a better understanding of my perspective. The Scriptures I hold to be sacred represent a cultural stockpile, a metaphorical (and spiritual) watershed from which centuries of meaningful human experiences have been derived – due in no small part to them being the product of millennia of such experiences. And yet, these very Scriptures entail a temporal cold war against all worldly beauty and freedom. Pleasure and wealth are to be shunned as corrupting forces, and thus it can be difficult to draw a line between the literal aesthetics foundationally described in the Old Testament, the realization of them as well as our own imaginings, and the *Prime Directive* of worldly rejection and self-denial. Judeo-Christian culture clearly exists on a spectrum of aesthetics iterated-upon over time. It seems intuitive to me that the golden mean here is neither the *beige fascism* of the most extreme sects of Protestantism nor the auric pomp and authoritarianism of universal churches. And such a golden mean is needed otherwise culture becomes directionless: guided merely by the industrial pursuit of pleasure-for-profit, and with erratic-at-best humanitarian awareness.

The world must be treated as a means to an end, even by the secular. It matters little for practical purposes how the end in question is described. The moment any worldly object or aspect becomes an end unto itself, everything downstream becomes a rational question of mechanical efficiency, and humanitarian collapse is a foregone conclusion. Here again, the (now hopefully) familiar stench of utilitarianism comes wafting. In the positively Utopian sense, it is of little harm to a society that any minority of its members are free to disbelieve in God, but atheistic thinking in power will always result in Machiavellian tyranny by way of sheer effectiveness. The secular ethicist is in some ways the most arrogant of all impostors: a would-be philosopher king able only to appeal to virtues which for them can exist only as abstract symbols. Even Platonic virtue has its ultimate roots in religious experience. Any leader of mankind, and this goes similarly for political leaders as cultural and so on, must either fear God in their own way, or the rest of us must understand that we are dealing with a person who fashions themselves as something derivative of a god, perhaps not omnipotent or omniscient in their own minds, but sufficiently above the awareness of others to assume administration over them: a Supreme Ego. Obviously we cannot know for a fact what occurs in the minds of other people, but if it is not also obvious, I am not speaking to them or for them: I am speaking for myself, and I am speaking to you – a forgotten practice in these times of digital ego shrines and empty signaling.

Attempting to define beauty is just about the height of intellectual conceit; so here goes… I would define beauty as an expression of intricacy that goes indefinitely beyond the rational bounds of efficiency without sacrificing efficiency itself. There is not a universal standard of beauty; beauty is however universal in the sense that all beauty exists within its own context. The beauty that exists within Nature, for example, is in every perceivable case an entropy-defying elegance that stands in contrast to the mechanical background from which it emerges. It may exist *within the eye of the beholder*, but that beholding will be an expression of timelessness or a something similar. Beauty is a kind of unfolding mystery, like the universe itself, an abstract form that speaks to an order or intelligence beyond mechanical happenstance, or at the very least, beyond our current understanding. It defies our understanding by its presence, its extension in time. Nature is our first teacher of beauty, but we begin to *outgrow* the forms of our *spiritual youth* and seek a higher order – as if such a thing must surely exist – and we must do this, especially now; otherwise, we will never culturally escape from the ghetto, the endless simulation and dissimulation of the postmodern crisis. Nature will always be there as the aesthetic foundation, but it too, more than anything else, is, and must be, a means to an end.

Freedom has already been well-defined by people far more intelligent than I. The way I see it, the very concept of freedom-as-liberty is self-defeating, painting every anarchistic conversation into an all-too-familiar corner. But freedom-as-autonomy is oppressive when applied to others. "You are free only insofar as I say you are free", whereas an autonomous individual says "I am free because I can make choices." As soon as freedom becomes about a reservation of control decided by another mind or completely unfettered fulfillment of bodily impulses, choice itself becomes a superfluous concept – all actions become necessarily rational, inevitable. So how do we resolve this impasse? There is no easy answer, I'm afraid, because the very notion that this is something to be resolved is an exercise in hubris. We do this often. We see a problem, we perceive it as a collective problem, because it would not be perceived as a 'problem' (in the larger sense) at all if it were limited to a single individual, and our underdeveloped sense of self leads us to the conclusion that such a problem must be addressed socially or politically. The problem then becomes an intellectual trap unsolvable within its own logos. This is neither an easy point to make, nor to hear, but the vast majority of what we lovingly refer to as *issues* are mere distractions – exacerbated by mass media and our own personal insecurities.

Whether you believe that another person is a perpetrator of injustice or a victim of it, your ability to solve that problem for them is, in virtually every case, misguided. In the case of the victim, you will merely end up replacing their perpetrator, as their being a victim in the first place had more to do with their nature than the nature or status of anyone who victimized them, and you do not alter that; and in the case of the perpetrator, either you will end up serving them unwittingly because they were never a suitable enemy for you to engage (for example, the case of state corruption), or your defeat of them will prove that the problem was never collective, endemic, or catastrophic to begin with – an easy pill to swallow were it not for the sheer size of the average modern ego. This is not to say that the impulse to help others, in various contexts, is misguided, quite the contrary, but like all things with real power, there is potential for real danger. At times, the very impulse itself is where the sin begins, as it starts with an immediate distraction from one's own lot and reflexive judgment of another's, things we cannot truly understand. But we cannot then go running to the opposite extreme and become solipsistic monks unwilling or unable to act consequentially in the world. This is the metaphysical tension caused by our transition from a social collective to social individuals. There is a rather terrifying gray area for a moral conscience where selflessness and selfishness are no longer suitable analogs for right and wrong. The many artificial moral universes created in recent decades in the world of fiction exhibit this tension, sometimes with humorous effect.

The thing about morality: it does not merely shape the behavior of the individual, for the individual is in possession of thumbs, tools, and a microbiome – morality shapes the world.

To put things more simply and generally: we want to live in a world which is beautiful, even though our personal conceptions of it differ, and we want to have the freedom to make choices with our behavior, which naturally encounters the hard boundary of that same freedom granted to others. In my opinion, this essence is captured in the American cultural symbol of The Pursuit of Happiness. The importance of this symbol is its necessary individualism. Happiness is not framed as a responsibility of the state, on the contrary; the state is framed as an implicit obstacle to self-determination. The same is true of freedom. It is an understanding, a *public faith*, that the logical extension of moral adulthood is a culture of self-governance and therefore a state apparatus that is minimal-in-scope, perhaps even irrelevant as Marx (unoriginally) envisioned.

Ideally, we are hardest on ourselves, less so on our loved ones, less so on our neighbors, and so on away from our sphere of direct influence, and in this simple order, the world may learn to breathe again; any reversal of this order is a form of tyranny. It is a thing we must learn and master, otherwise tyranny is inevitable, at every scale. In this way, it matters little what kind of civic structure we build – its architecture – as long as we keep active this intuition about right and wrong in regards to the role of the state. To draw an analogy: when helping those in our lives whom we care for or in being helped, it rarely matters if no one involved is any kind of professional or academic expert in such things. A little intuition goes a long way with faith – the kind that wordlessly reassures us of the value of the people in our lives, whoever they may happen to be. Just being present and genuinely caring (the kind of thing no scientific instrument could measure): it is the latent human superpower that moves mountains and heals the sick.

If I love my neighbor as myself, and he loves me in turn, then we have just made government between the two of us obsolete. This can extend theoretically outward to within the bounds of human cultural reason. We will not realize the perfect, but we will reach for it. What else, reach for second-best?

This will take time, and I imagine will be a virtual impossibility for the modern urban population, but I welcome nothing more than surprise in this regard, and I know the human is capable – I have seen it! Again, the alternative is the Boot: the darkest of all dark ages. It is not the State of Nature that anyone should fear. I would be infinitely more afraid of being anchored to any major city, wondering which hour would be the last: when the lights go and do not come back, and the water stops running. At least when rats flee a sinking ship, they have an easier time climbing over each other.

We do not need to think of ourselves as Christian per se, if the notion of being a Christian feels beneath your person. We can merely think of ourselves as adults. Must we involve a third-party authority to settle a conflict between us? What an embarrassing failure that would be! What a demonstration of our mutual impotence and idiocy! It is tempting to become like the idolaters and treat all conflict as a heteronymous card game, deriving from a set of meaningless symbols, where one of us necessarily wins and the other loses. One need not fall back on their own weakness but can pull levers on a much larger machine, becoming a mouthpiece for a vocabulary that is not their own. It is the original and ultimate form of "selling out". The Empire never has to break such sellouts; they see power, they covet. They see a game, they play. And there is a certain sinking feeling, which I know cannot be unique to me, that one feels upon witnessing another person stoop to playing the silly game instead of participating in humanity, as if they have been replaced by an imposter or body-snatcher. It is the corporate ladder mentality at large. Such people see no difference between the kind of intelligence that produces the Sistine Chapel, that imparts meaning to everything that we experience, and the kind that seeks out a piece of cheese at the center of a maze.

So the state wants us atomized? Very well then. Allow me to introduce you to this thing called atomic energy. If everyone of appropriate age were to take responsibility for their own actions at all times, to accept the non-negotiability of moral law, for their own sake if nothing else, not only is the state instantly defanged, but a number of other "social issues" will find expedient (and humane) resolution. A politician (or corporate officer for that matter) does not have power because their name is on a plaque; they have power because the chain of command ends with a spiked ball – not a person but an object, for they have whored out their soul from 8:30-5:00, Monday to Friday, and they either have no moral compass to speak of or have come to believe that there is some special dispensation for sins committed on the clock. The ziggurat is crowded with unambitious prostitutes. There is no way around this, no system, no number of summary executions that can steal us away from the individual burden of moral responsibility. This fact is a threat both to the state and statism.

It was right for Oppenheimer to feel remorse, and it is also right for the rest of us to forgive him and everyone else involved in the Project. The forgiveness is a demonstration of understanding: that none of us are self-created and that knowledge and circumstance may be all that stands between any one of us and becoming the next dark angel fallen beyond redemption. I can with great ease and conviction either defend *or* condemn him. The human condition is fraught with turmoil and contradiction, and the true content of the inner self is ultimately *unintelligible* to others. This does not preclude the concept of truth, quite the contrary; it forces us to confront our moral universe alone, which is to say, among other things, that Oppenheimer is just a symbol in this case and no more remarkable as a subject of moral inspection than you or myself. I could have used Einstein, for example, but the angle would be far less recognizable. Einstein got off light (get it?). The real problem is the degree to which all of this evocation dissolves once scientific progress serves exclusively the interests of state and/or globalized industry. How can I be inspired by the martyrdom of Marie Curie if, in the end, the entire institution she served was never meant for any higher purpose than effective mass production of weapons of war and consumable goods? The streets named after her seem like hollow memorials given the gap between the perception of *what science has given us* and the reality of all the *real stuff* existing far beyond the reach, let alone the understanding, of the typical consumer and belonging exclusively to the commercial or industrial domains: a gated community that no one enters by accident, at least not anymore. What I mean is that her martyrdom is effectively (retrospectively) for the state and not for any ideal of advancing human knowledge, since the benefits of such knowledge are well out of the reach of the average citizen. But as always, serve the emperor well and you will be celebrated, whether you did so out of love or ambition. The typical dollar you spend is on a product engineered with great intent to be cheap to produce in massive quantities while holding as little value over time as possible for the end user – quite effectively designed to impoverish anyone who exchanges their wealth for it. You can even include food into this category. The whole Solvay Conference of 1927 might as well be spinning in their graves; either that or, for ethical consistency, we should be pissing on them. Every scientific advancement of the 20th century might as well be a big *who-cares* outside of Penicillin, if we're to have a technocratic caste system; then it truly was just another Will to Power, in this case by yet another class that I do not belong to, and I should be no more inspired by it than Louis XIV's famous proclamation of "L'État, c'est moi." *Good for you!*

Technology & Theosophy

I have endured your insolence long enough, oh technological terror construct. I have lived in the shadow of your foreboding filth and suffered from your automated abandonment. In all of your godless and avaricious ways, I have been an afterthought. I have fallen through the cracks in your false façade – the North Korean storefront that is your multifarious and unaccountable policies, jurisdictions, and social engineers, and in such dim corners of the world, I found other afterthoughts. But the worst toleration of all was that of your mediocrity. You, who lied to us all about your power as you lied about the power of God. But God is unharmed by your blasphemy. It is your own self-aggrandizement that rings especially pitiful.

The value of all technology is a function of its efficiency. Full stop. No matter what piece of technology you hold in your hand, be it a wooden stick or a PKE meter, its status as such is not a series of points but of degrees. The most damning realization about our technology-obsessed world is the sheer wastefulness of our devices and industrial processes. The paradigm of mass production is a Faustian bargain that ensures the mediocrity of consumer goods. *More* people having technology, as opposed to fewer people having *better* technology, is a net-loss in quality of life over a sufficient time scale, once the inefficiency of the technology multiplied by population-use reaches a critical mass. An easy and immediate example is the proliferation of lithium batteries and the devices they power. Globalized industry coupled with sociopathic marketing has sold an alarming number of consumers on a sector of industry that will, when all is said and done, have contributed far more to the landfill and metal poisoning of nations than their wealth. Meanwhile, all those involved in the manufacturing process, from extraction of raw materials, to logistics, to assembly of parts, will turn a guaranteed profit with the aid of international governments and equally-manufactured public consent.

The highest tier of human technology is (necessarily) used to produce lower tiers. What separates the tiers is not capability per se, but efficiency and scale. It all abstracts to time-in and time-out. It may seem like an obvious good that we produce more technology for more people, but the incentives that develop over time in a global-industrial marketplace drive down the quality of consumer technology while furthering the expansion of manufacturing capacity. The most profitable products will never be of the highest quality (least of all in a marketplace where the potential customer base encompasses all of mankind); this was evident to Adam Smith when he described the division of labor; the problem, as with many things, is the runaway of scale and complexity: where the overhead becomes an end unto itself and the waste becomes *more than we can stomach* – itself a capricious phenomenon subject to manipulation by mass media. We have been conditioned to stomach too much.

The division of labor has become global. Some are designated producers (slaves), others are designated consumers (also slaves). Consumers now may only become Owners through tremendous effort at proving oneself *loyal to the Empire* either by climbing the ranks of a sufficiently-large organization or by creating a product that can be bought by a sufficiently-large organization thereby systematically shifting long-term assets into the hands of the owning class (and keeping them there). The icing on top of this technocratic cake is the fruitless argument the state prescribes to the proles between capitalism and socialism (see: Right versus Left). Rhetoric and theatrical debate are taught in public schools as a legitimate intellectual tool and pastime – no doubt resembling the sophistry of the ancient world. I am not without sin in this regard! I have played both sides – genuinely too! But I had the naïve mutation of actually wanting to get at the Truth, whatever that is, and so I found myself eventually alienated from any artificial social group with which I connected. It is all clichéd nonsense: a card game of selective amnesia reinforced by state media. It is time we humbled ourselves and not pass this sin on to our children. Rest assured: nothing allowed on state media or approved (even passively) by state media is actually a threat to the state. At best, it can be an aesthetic distraction, whose long term purpose is to be defeated, ridiculed, or otherwise appropriated. And to be clear: we are living in a global-industrial-banking state; if you can access it with a credit card, it falls under the umbrella of *state media*. The point here is that the abstraction of 'product' is applied everywhere, and a similar division of labor designates producers of state-commodified ideas for complimentary consumers. Controlled opposition, that is we all.

To be an actual player anywhere in mass media, one must have a product to sell. Any purpose contrary to profit is either commodified, abandoned, or destroyed utterly by various selection forces. Many have tried and failed to leverage a deal with the devil and sell their commodity with practiced bravado, hoping to play both sides, shielded by ambiguity. But this is a line one can only walk aesthetically and never ethically. Eventually cross-purposes must be resolved, a singular master chosen. One cannot remain true to themselves and also survive in an environment that requires the opposite. We all compromise, but all compromises have limits.

How would you go about showing-off human technology to an alien civilization? Does is occur to you that you have no earthly way of doing that? You may show them your toys. That which one might put up for cosmic catalog is well beyond your reach. And what you can show them is so plagued by software errors and planned obsolescence that any knowledgeable user would be too embarrassed for demonstration, and that is all before even considering the labor-resource cost of the overall manufacture and its long-term consequences. The real reason aliens will not talk to you is out of compassion: to spare you the chagrin. You have everything to learn from them and nothing to offer. And they have the awkward task of cataloging the human race and having to decide if it makes more sense to do so individually, statistically, or sentimentally.

When visitors from another world made contact with our leaders, they saw two things: they saw our leaders for what they really are, and they saw that the rest of us did not.

If an advanced alien civilization, as we truly understand the concept, did make contact with *us*, it would only be to absorb us into their much larger galactarian hegemony, and it is not difficult to see why.

The greatest failure of modern socialists is their focus on money instead of technology, which is doubly embarrassing given their core ideation of "the means of production". It seems to me that they are more concerned with the *ends* of production. And their confusion has *trickled down* to the modern proletariat, who believe that they are (and are believed to be) bourgeoisie, but they lack the aesthetic and technological sophistication – the equipment – to have any meaningful power in their own right. Their power is virtual, like most of their technology: completely abstracted behind symbolic interfaces. It is like magic to them. And when the exploits of the owning class filter down to them, they are shocked if anything, and cling to plausible deniability as an opiate for their sense of powerlessness, however numbed. In truth, it is the same now as it was in the high middle ages, only with an expanded set of symbols, different aesthetics.

We must decide, individually, what role technology will play in our lives. (The collective comes later, in aggregate, not before.) I refer back to idealistic Star Trek: consider the efficient-uniformity, shall we say, of the devices used by all characters of a particular faction. Characters have varying knowledge and interest in technology, but all are comfortable and competent in using it, and the tech itself is not a multitude of mass-produced consumables but a logical array of the best generational designs for discrete purposes. Newer designs improve upon older, because anything else would be illogical, same with the production processes as well. The true *socialism* of Star Trek is technological, not economical – right down to the matter replicator that enables the whole utopia! This simple vision is the only sort of role technology can have where our personal power and identity is retained. The alternative is a more focused retreat from technology, and eventual acceptance of a quality of life with more physical labor and fewer distractions. The notion that technology should empower those entirely ignorant of its design is the slipperiest of all slippery slopes – essentially to say that it *should* be as magic – and can only lead to a sociological dead end where even individuality itself is a privilege of the highest class. And that would be a great deal of time spent and ground covered to end up in the exact same existential place as ever.

This is the temporal migration, and it must occur because in this place we are out of time. Those that remain will be oppressed by the future. They will conglomerate, themselves lost.

This is not to say, however, that there are only two possible directions. We are surrounded by an ocean of theoretically infinite undiscovered countries. But not all destinations are created equal, and every journey begins with a choice; those that remain are merely those that fail to choose. Those that fail to choose, in all times and places, become slaves.

Technology is the only material demonstration of power. Everything else that can be communicated about is merely symbolic in nature. The illusion of technological progress is maintained with aesthetic sleight-of-hand. The public generally perceives this progress because their *toys* continue to improve, but only incrementally, and never in a way that actually empowers them beyond the ability to allocate increasing amounts of their time to these distractions that effectively funnel their attention. The most common example that I know of is "smartphones" and their digital cameras. The amount of R&D and marketing sophistry that goes into the manufacture and sale of these cameras is staggering when one considers profitable end use to be such an edge minority case compared to unproductive diversion. Is this the height of progress with which I am supposed to be enamored, that photos of oneself and one's pets gain in resolution each calendar year? Or should I be taken aback by upper class creative dilettantes and their shameless self-promotion that never has to answer to real market competition for quality or efficiency? Subtract the social media cave, and all that remains is decades of money-laundering and egoistical time-wasting.

Artificial Intelligence, as the term is commonly used today, is the next gimmick on the conveyor belt. It is being marketed as a kind of magic, which should be a massive red flag in a scientific world, but goes largely parroted regardless by the consumer populace, reinforced by mass media of course. The current iteration of AI is a direct result of the virtual mountain range of data that has been collected by the technocratic class, and their inevitable need to sift through it, which no quantity of human beings could ever manage at animal speeds. This data, at least in their eyes, is the sum-total of human thought, as regurgitated en masse by the internet-connected population of mankind, and all they need do in order to achieve godhood is to construct an *overmind* that can bring to bear all of these thoughts in simultaneity. Novelties like ChatGPT can easily be thought of as *open beta* tests that they release to the proles, merely a watered-down application of the *real thing* which we, the consumer public, will likely never see[10] – the ultimate purpose of the test being, like everything else, more data collection. *What are the limits of what they will tolerate, accept, celebrate?* We fall right into the delusion that these technological novelties are for us. Why? Do you really believe that this massive, unfeeling machine works for you? What do you own? Take a good look at that cash in your wallet, if you still even carry currency; whose name and inscription is that?

---

[10] What we would "see" would only be a 'Wizard of Oz' illusion.

The most glaring problem with AI is that, outside of fiction and casual conversation, no one seems to be stopping to ask "Why?" Why is it desirable to create a fully-automated world, a *permanent vacation* world? Society is already more automated than it has ever been. Tell me, do you feel powerful, more at ease? Virtually nothing we build or design to be automated works as efficiently or reliably as its manual counterpart, where applicable. This is certainly not where automation began, but we stand now overlooking the end, where the *Jenga tower* has become far too top-heavy to remain standing for long. What use could there possibly be to concerns about something like minimum wage or workplace safety when all technological trajectory is aiming us toward a thoroughly unemployed future, which will resemble the past more than anyone in media is even prepared to confront, let alone admit. The average consumer talks as if some new magic is manifesting on the planet, and yet computer science has not fundamentally changed at all. We are being sold on a future where programmers are carried about on algorithmic thrones like the pharaohs of old, having completed their *Great Work* and permanently establishing their station. This will last until they grow too fat and ignorant, and their underlings will start the last 3,500 years over again.

What is the abstract here? Is the dream to build a world where no one has to work again? Is there even *a dream*? Blind idealism is at least more respectable than mere blindness. God has gone out of style, but this *godlike thing* truly excites people? To what end? I cannot ask this question enough. There is a bright-eyed credulity in people that they seem afraid to question. It does not stand up to scrutiny. It is so weak and baseless that any assault against it is viewed with an "oh, how could you?" affectation as if one were mugging a child. The world tires of hearing what it has never bothered to listen to. And this credulity must be defeated, painful as it is. The light burns our eyes because we've never used them. Our technology must have a conscious paradigm of some kind, must reflect our inner values and purpose; otherwise, the mindless momentum of global consumerism, digital marketing, and industrial statism will lead us into a dead end: a dark age unlike any prior. The fact is that technology always reflects its purpose as a matter of ontology, and so our ultimate problem here, as always, is moral – because you cannot successfully measure human progress in GHz.

Both the collapse of European monarchies and the advent of the Scientific Revolution of the 17th century caused massive disruptions to world power structures that have since either rebranded or been replaced by new ones. The future is beginning, and will continue, to look more like the past as we understand it with power (in the form of resources, knowledge, technology, or military) concentrated into a minority of the species with the vast majority having little economic value beyond that of a serf. This will happen not by civil law but by natural law. The systematic replacement of design with automation, of engineering with sales and marketing, and of education with state indoctrination will lead to a top-heavy aristocracy of dealers and clients, the average consumer along-for-the-ride at-best, and to some extent this has already taken place. Market forces exert corrective pressure locally (and every once in a while, an individual gets a say), but such forces are canceled out at the global scale, where even the most casual cooperation (read: conspiracy) between industrial competitors outweighs the merely symbolic power of bureaucratic governments, themselves reliant on the very products or services they are called to arbitrate, not to even mention tax revenue. This produces a circle-jerk of global proportions where, to put it bluntly, the average prole believes that they have both power and knowledge that they have never and could never put to use. The lie is easier for them to bear than the truth, because, quite simply, far more is demanded of them in today's world than mere physical labor and discomfort. Their minds are more subjugated than their bodies: the automation of tyranny.

This, I believe, brings us to the *elephant in the room*, or for the materialist: the "man in the sky". While the cat is away, the mice will play, as they say, and played they have. The common ridicule of monotheism has become, as I have already touched upon, quite unsophisticated, betraying more about those doing the ridicule than their target. This leaves the average prole, already inundated with data of varying importance, metaphysically blinded. This is to say: as long as religion can remain *ridiculous*, at best another category of human aesthetic interest, then there is no longer any force in human civilization calling the information creature to consciousness, no otherworldly demand for action or choice, no aspiration beyond social conformity and homeostasis. There remain only biological needs and the fulfillment of those needs: human nature is reduced to the complexity of Ohm's Law. *Man lives on bread alone.*

I thought I might do something here with the three Temptations, but gimmicks are unbecoming of such serious discussion. Surely Dostoevsky did a better job with that already. Nineteenth century Europe did not have a greater prophet. But it seems like all prophets, he existed not for warning but for glory, for few alive have faith sufficient to be warned by a living prophet. They may read, and even venerate, the scripture of prophets past, but when the Word stares them presently in the face, they do not recognize Him. Dostoevsky's words *are* read, however, every day in multiple languages, and if they are not prophecy, they surely did predict the future of the human condition as we know it. The peculiar part, to me, is how ironically irrelevant technology turns out to be in the end. Technologically, our world today is radically different from his; theologically however, as if it was just last week.

We are rationally assured, by many channels of data, that our sensory faculties have been calibrated by millions of years of evolutionary history. It should be trivial to state that our perception of time is likewise, but we do not seem to acknowledge this, at least not aesthetically, if perhaps ethically or mathematically. By energetic standards, we are quite slow, and by cosmic standards, quite transient. This understanding should make certain people very afraid. The abstract notion of time becomes a barrier between thoughts – a *plausible deniability* whereby events that were (or are) *sufficiently far away*, as if on the other *side* of the universe, need only be acknowledged with extraordinary evidence, effectively precluding choice. The fact is, just as the universe is under no obligation to be intelligible to you, neither is it obliged to *tick* at a rate you would find intuitive. We may possess many reliable means to sample the world and graph its trajectory, but to supplant the pursuit of Truth with the pursuit of mere data is an exercise in arrogance, like skipping to the end of a story because you think you understand the point, missing it entirely.

A world *where no one need work* is, intentionally or not, an outright scam. A great deal of human work has already been undertaken, resources exhausted to build the fully-automatic utopia, and this work will be repaid. Those with the skills to maintain the machines will find themselves gainfully, if not exhaustively, employed. The rest, if not among the owning class, will subsist on the carrying capacity of these machines, which will be ruthless in their materialistic calculus. You fear for the current state of the healthcare or legal systems? Just wait until automated vending machines are adapted to those industries too! Have a problem with one of the robots? Call this number where another robot will "attempt" to help you. Layer upon layer of software abstraction and waste heat production just to obscure the fact that your time and/or money are already gone, and the thing you purchased is not as you thought. Behind every door you can open will be an empty room with an unswept floor.

In this metaphysical position, one is trapped in time, like a rat trapped in a dead end of a maze, having lost the previously indefatigable drive to seek out the object of their eternal desire – their reason to live. One rat does this, and we call it a mental illness; a whole civilization does this, and we call it a dark age. One wonders how it actually *happens*. The truth is: one day at a time. It never officially begins because such things implicate denial and decline, and it never really ends either – one day, someone is conscious enough (and perhaps literate enough) to proclaim a certain period of the past greatly inferior, encouraged by a comparative lack of productive or creative human activity. You don't really know that you were asleep until after you have awoken. The point here is that one does not drown in quicksand all at once, and what our history cannot unequivocally tell you is that the true darkness of what we call a dark age is not a lack of technological progress or personal liberty but a great recession of human consciousness. The other aspects of civilization are downstream of this, not upstream.

Metaphorically speaking, the alien, the angel, represents the compartmentalized self-awareness of Western Man: on the outside looking in at himself, a thing at-once familiar and entirely foreign. In truth, extraterrestrial life could take on a multitude of exotic forms, but we do not overly care to imagine that. We prefer not simply intelligent life but *intelligible* life. So be it. Prefer you the angel or the alien, I suppose it matters not. But think as often as necessary on your alien (or angelic) houseguest and what it would be to show them your world. This is the last gasp of those who fail to nurture their consciousness, their soul. That symbol will do if it is all you have because this is too important – either to ignore or to emasculate with irony. And no one you can see on that little device of yours can tell you what to do or give you the answer, for in this murk we are all equals in blindness. The only way to avoid being led by the blind is to open your eyes.

Materialism is a tool. A materialist is a tool. It is all they can ever be. You can create a tool, you can use a tool, or you can destroy a tool, but you cannot appeal to the spirit of a tool. A tool cannot be reasonable, it can only be rational. It has no free will of its own, only natural consequences it can follow. A tool cannot be baptized in, with, or by water. It is saved only with maintenance and proper use, and even then, eventually succumbs to corruption by the elements. A tool cannot have an existential crisis; its existence was complete at the final moment of manufacture. From that point on, it began to break down, however slowly. Neither can a tool have an existential breakthrough. It will, again, simply function until it can do so no longer, at which point it will be repaired until it can be repaired no longer. A tool is responsible for nothing. A tool cannot create, it can only duplicate, and with diminishing returns. To become a tool is a one-way trip; but for the grace of God, one does not return. But a tool does have a purpose, and the more useful it is, the more it is cared for. It is not so different than being a slave, and there is an often-overlooked security in slavery. It is far more natural to the human condition than our all-too-Western hypocrisy allows us to admit. It has always been the voice of God calling us to rise above our voluntary servitude to worldly technology and wield the technology of heaven.

All this being the case, tell me: are you a tool? Do you want to be? Are you sure? If your final answer is truly yes, then I at least congratulate you on making your first choice. *May you be alive at the end of the world!*

Psychedelic Society & Its Future

If you have made it this far, then you have gained enough experience to finish the game.

Buy the ticket, take the ride.[11]

Two degenerate aesthetics:

Every person is virtually identical, but all more terrified of each other than of God. Their scripture is full of color and wisdom, but their minds know only fear and scorn. They are one body: existing only for the body, mindless limbs grasping at a world of darkness, forever.

Every person is slightly different, but all are self-absorbed and inebriated to an unbecoming degree. Their music speaks of love and otherworldly curiosity, but they wallow in hatred of their enemies and believe only in the goods of this world. They are many bodies: existing only for the body, masters of their own hell, slaves to themselves.

I believe with limited effort that the vast majority of mankind can come together in agreement *at least* on this basis. This is a rough illustration of the two-dimensional spectrum of freedom to which we have been subjected by recorded history. Whatever the particulars of a *new* kind of society we entertain, we can at least agree that we do not want something that resembles either of these extremes; that is, of a spiritual society.[12] I am not here to suggest yet another mockery of the kingdom of God, such as the like I have criticized in this very work; this is not a proposal of revolution; this is an emergency floatation device, and a map to a deserted island with a buried stockpile of goods and treasure, where the storm will not pass over and no demon dare tread.

---

[11] Note to self

[12] The extremes of a materialist society, I hope, I do not need to reiterate at this point.

The devil cannot create; he can only imitate or destroy. He may memorize and gamble, but he cannot see the future. His servants memorize the present, reach into the past, imitate dead glories, and gamble with people's lives, so we shall reach into the future and migrate to where he cannot see.

Media is the first enemy of the postmodern psychedelic emigrant. It is the first layer of simulation that you can see. There is a silver lining, however; the beauty of the postmodern lies in its variety and unpredictability. Not all media is without value, and a shrewd consumer may cultivate a stream of useful information. The second enemy is overreaction, to run from one robotic state to another with oppositional aesthetics and hard rules. This is a trap whereby one's identity is only defined negatively by its opposition, and so cannot even exist on its own. Many such dead ends exist in the gigantic sphere of media available for consumption today and the synthetic human identities peddled by it.

Why psychedelic? Frankly, because the word "spiritual" has become too diffuse and I lack a better word with similar specificity. I would, however, suggest we create a new symbol, to advance beyond the implied frivolity of the mid-20th century Western golden age. But the important thing is that it is merely a symbol and that what I am gesturing at is something beyond the words, however intelligible. It is not my intention to evoke specific imagery, of kaleidoscopic colors, Fabergé patterns, and mindless self-indulgence, though such imagery comes to mind for a reason. To view the psychedelic as nothing more than the empty aesthetic is the equivalent of viewing religion as nothing more than a set of words and clothing. These things are incidental. Where Spirit goes, there creativity and power will always follow, and that creative power causes a *Cambrian Explosion* within that sphere. From there, one gets derivative forms that vary in their qualitative distance from the *true vine*. We like to place such explosions within a category we can grasp because we think it is we who are doing this, or that if we can place something in a box we then gain possession of it, but this inspiration is beyond us and we merely play a part in a larger scheme, which lends validity to the saying "Time makes fools of us all."

So to reverse the negative momentum of civilized stagnation, first a break with cultural cynicism and arrogance is required. We must surrender the mindset that we share with the doomed ancient Greeks: that we have *seen it all before, been there, done that,* etc. It is a conceit that naturally arises from intellectualism and philosophy: as long as there are 'experts', or people whose occupation it is to *figure out* reality, there must be people who believe they understand how the world works in a significant-enough totality to justify teaching others about it. You simply cannot have one without the other, unless this is all just some complicated and meaningless dance. We cannot all be equals while some of us are *more equal than others* in a way that only inconsistently stands up to scrutiny. The king cannot fulfill his role while behaving as the equal of his subjects; it would be a lie on some level or another – at least within an individualistic paradigm, which is how we view the world typically today, in the West.[13] Neither can we desperately reach back into the merely symbolic past in search of an idealized end state, for those states were not ends unto themselves, and can only change over time as with all temporal things, or in all likelihood, lead us back to where currently stand. Embalming a corpse only causes it to decompose more slowly.

---

[13] Both the European Absolutism of the high middle ages and the Great Chain of Being prior to that demonstrate pre-individualistic human organization, at least in thinking. History seems more barbaric to us the further back in time we look due to consciousness becoming less collective over time. For example, a small village stoning one of its citizens to death would be unthinkable in today's world, but the ancient world was not simply more violent as much as more collectivistic, not unlike a body's immune system attacking cancerous tissue; or if viewed negatively, someone cutting their own flesh. In the ancient days of the Law, this was divine and necessary justice, today it would be nothing but murder. Such rigidity is needed to socially engineer a population that lives more according to the body, and we see the same ruthless proportion from all state apparatus globally and historically (taking the place of God).

Religion, Technology, and Culture: these are the prime attributes of a coherent civilization. Everything else is a means to one or more of these ends or a derivative of one or more of these beginnings, starting first and foremost with religion, when one goes back far enough. One may be tempted to consider religion within the category of culture, but there is a reason I separate them, however much all three interact. These three must be in balance and complement each other. When this is not the case, social cohesion starts to break down and overall net wealth decreases. The goal of a statist society, as the name manages to imply, seeks the establishment of a static program of these elements, with the thinking that a clever enough code will beget something akin to perpetual motion. Thus far, the cleverest programs have remained stable for centuries at most.[14]

Why is this? I suppose there are many factors, but I believe it breaks down to two things: change and choice. These are fundamental tenets of life. Life has no nature without change and no quality without choice, no purpose. To construct a civilization meant to merely function as a giant body – a corpus – is to imminently become an enemy, *the* enemy, of existing life. You will have to contend with life almost immediately, the moment you separate yourself from it: its tendency to multiply, divide, and perpetually change; you will enable these things as often as resist them in order to assert and maintain control.

---

[14] However long they last, it is important to keep in mind that when they fail, they fail catastrophically, at great human cost.

If we are to have a state, something like it, or a society of organized intent, then we must think like the gardener. You can build a trellis or plant a row of seeds, but life has its own way and each lifeform contains a nonzero potential for divergence from expectation. At every moment of divergence, the design is faced with the choice of accommodation or destruction. A gardener favors the health of the garden above that of any single lifeform, but not that of all lifeforms. A gardener favors mutation that increases the quality of the fruit or longevity of the plant, but not mutation for its own sake. A tree is not wet concrete to be poured into any mold, but a tree *can* be pruned, grafted, and restrained to a compromise in its shape. Life is no different. It exists suspended between the environment and the intent of all creatures within it. Life is like fire, it can be stoked or snuffed out, but is ultimately an ascendant force that defies material restraint – the more restrained it is, the less it can be said to exist at all.

Psychedelic society is not something I am proposing so much as something I am attempting to describe. It is something accessed perennially, perpetually, by certain individuals and families. It would be fair, if a bit controversial, to say that what I am gesturing at is the *true life*, the actual party, or true civilization that has been eking out its existence with great disinterest about (to borrow a phrase from the Jehovah's Witnesses) *Satan's doomed system of things*. This thing we now call "civilization" is more akin to a mold that has spread out of control.

Enter Clownworld.

I do not want to dwell on the infinite ways I can satirize Clownworld. I want to dwell on the obvious-in-hindsight purpose of *all this*, that is to say, life. We act as though it is a deep philosophical question, but a man reaches more-or-less the age of thirty and it starts to become clear. The purpose of life is family, and the purpose of family is children. The first and last victims of our iniquity, our mediocrity, our corruption, are children and childhood.

I think a truly fulfilling society will be ordered around the fact that childhood is sacred and beautiful, as well as the acknowledgement that every adult has an inner-child that is as much a part of their person as all the experiences that have occurred to them since. It is not a period of inferiority that is to be overcome as quickly as possible. It is in fact a more ideal state of being that is finite because of the temporality of this world. Adulthood is more akin to a spiked carapace one adopts as a means of defense – a damning reflection upon the environment that produces it. But of course, how silly does such a mindset render much of the business of our technocracy? To a child, our world looks either silly or incomprehensible. The perspectives of children should always be reflected upon, even and especially when they are offensive or dismissible to us.

This is NOT to gesture at a kind of "childish" civilization. For in fact, what we are stuck in now is an extremely childish one. Quite the contrary: it takes exceptional maturity and godliness to be the best possible keepers and parents of children. Our state treats children, ours or others', like roadkill. They'll scrape their corpses off the asphalt, but the Great Highway Project must continue. So to compensate for all the wounds and casualties, we try to artificially extend childhood. It is a degenerate cycle: life exists for the sake of living as large as possible and as long as possible, and if the weak and small among us, whose minds cannot assimilate our world of sophistication and decadence, are harmed, then that is simply, as the young people of today might say, a *skill issue*.

I think what I am saying is very intuitive to a lot of people, which is why society does not simply implode the moment it strays from its peak.[15] People of every generation make sacrifices for their children, and most that reject the notion of family from adolescence eventually come around as they age and acquire some wisdom. Life continues on. The greatest embarrassment of every state in history: despite the greatest, bloodiest, and most expensive societies collapsing every few centuries or a millennium at most, humans continue on. *Life finds a way!* And that way is and has always been family and community[16]. It is time to wake up now. Old wisdom bears new repetition.

If we were living in a golden age utopia, even something vaguely like the world the Baby Boomers grew up in, it would be far more forgivable to stray from family and lose oneself in the *doomed system* – so many things to do, so much potential for individual power and distraction. I think this is why we have to forgive them. If their sin was thinking themselves so apart and entitled, do we then continue that sin by not considering that we might have been no different in their shoes? It is far from a comforting thought. We often cope with the present by projecting onto the past, but it is wrong. It robs us of an opportunity for self-awareness. And maybe that, after all, was the problem: resentment towards the Boomers usually centers on opportunity. Of all the opportunity they were surrounded by, it seems that it was overwhelmingly of an earthly order, and moments for spiritual progress were a narrow door through which only a few unknown souls managed to pass.

---

[15] Incidentally, this allows for my argument in the first place. If the only alternative to statism was atavism, then I would be a tremendous hypocrite, not to mention owe Hobbes an apology.

[16] It is important to emphasize the true conception of community: a group of people who live and work together. Virtual communities, or groups of people who share a common interest, while convenient for the sake of conversation, are superficial simulacra, and have lulled many impressionable people, especially the young, into a false sense of real human socialization or love, while all-too-often in reality they are entirely alienated from the real people around them (i.e. their family) and subsequently their culture, and struggle with some hostility to interact with personality types different from their own.

And this brings us to a second key facet of psychedelic society: it is without media. That is not to say without creativity in its infinite forms, again quite the contrary. But psychedelic society is never vicarious, centralized, or programmed. It is first-person and present. It does not need to gesture at a scriptural or martial authority, or a memory space of shared references. It gestures only at life and the felt presence of direct experience. This concept would be unpopular to anyone with desire for earthly power over others. Such a reorientation, fully realized, does something comparable to Marx's true communism whereby the state becomes obsolete. The fatal flaw in Marx's design, and his derivatives', is being materialistic they rely on using the state as a means to accomplish this, hence endless and costly failure. After everything the human race has endured on this Earth, that we can remember through story or science, what have you, ages of struggle against nature and each other and self, we should be (should've been) immediately hostile to any notion of dissolving the vehicle that got us here – however ramshackle it might appear at times. Who or what could forward such a notion but the enemy of all mankind?

So, materialist society creates a game for all to play, and the nature of children being small and ill-equipped to compete is really just an inconvenience. The goal is to prepare (read: indoctrinate) them as early as possible. The less innocence they have to look back on, the better. We care for them physically as long as necessary, but really they are in the way, and what they experience is of far less importance than the world of adult business. We will make it up to them later in the form of material decadence and pampered retirement. – In reality, our order is upside-down. The business of adulthood is and always has been the caretaking of children and the enrichment of family. As we become more top-heavy in our frivolity, we undermine the very thing we thought gave us license to do so in the first place. This is not to say that everyone must start a family, obviously that is less than ideal or even impossible in some cases; it is simply a matter of what lies at the core of our very purpose for stockpiling resources and organizing ourselves.

All human organizations that have either served as the state in a general sense or attempted to become the state[17] have led children into harm on an atrocious scale, either through neglect, deprivation, or direct abuse of their person. Every one of them from various daycares, to the USSR, to the Roman Catholic Church… none of them is without the worst kind of sin. *It would be better for them if they had not been born.* The likely response here is to quote statistics, the primary language of the state. But there are no words in the language of statistics to describe suffering or to evaluate a broken childhood. The irony is we enumerate dead or traumatized children and many other sorts of victims every single day, and yet as the cynical saying goes: *the death of one is a tragedy; the death of millions is just a statistic.* The numbers, being symbols, have only symbolic feeling, and we are left with an insipid theatre where often the most obvious crocodiles cry the most convincing tears. It is neither healthy nor helpful to suffer vicariously on behalf of strangers, but it is a symptom of a deep-seeded compromise: we truly do not know how to act properly, how to apply our village-brains to this one-world meat grinder where everything happens in the millions and billions. Add to that the ubiquity of psychoactive medication, and we are utterly divorced emotionally from the true state of things. You cannot be well-adjusted to this world without also being numb, and one comes to expect a degree of hostility at this assertion in turn, but I am saying nothing new.

---

[17] supplant generative social structures and traditions

Family is the only vehicle by which one can separate oneself from society without being completely alone. Solitude is essential for reflection on the human condition, but this is precisely a result of our condition being fundamentally social. We are becoming something, if not less-than-human, other-than-human, as a result of being atomized and indoctrinated by the state. There is no technological antidote to this, but insofar as the human is concerned, biology *is* technology. However, it is important to keep in mind that 'family' need not be limited to immediate biology. There are in fact even biological reasons for this, but more importantly, when one reaches a certain point of spiritual evolution, 'family' takes on a more abstract[18] nature. The essential point is that any other human organization is artificial, and no human organization is impotent.

Large-scale collapse is a baffling and deceptive thing. When an event is occurring everywhere, but not to the same extent everywhere, nor to the same extent at different points in the process, to the point where it is challenging to draw a clear box around a discrete event at all, communication about it is put under strain. Add to that differences in individual human motivation, investment, bias, culture, and intelligence, and one might as well forget any notion of social understanding. One will be lucky to find common understanding amongst one's immediate peers, and even then, it is not unlike staring down a food shortage. The greatest deception of social media is that there is any common understanding of human behavior or any true virtual community, as if human community itself is an interchangeable thing. It is comforting to think that one can predict the behavior and morality of others, attain kinship with anyone, or have a secular brotherhood of man, and it is easy to behave when there is plenty of food to go around, if you understand my inference. Like manslaughter on Black Friday, we have had many shameful warnings. As with the world, we feel more in control when we can place people in a series of predictable boxes, but those boxes depend upon a structure more ephemeral than anything previously made by human hands.

---

[18] Christian

We will see new horrors.[19] Some in the sense of devices and some as people themselves – freaks of artifice. In some cases, merely gross spectacles, in other, darker cases: monsters that give us pause. Neither case is something the state will ever protect you or your children from. They are a product of a sick civilization – in the same way that mental illness is a product of a sick household. It is the Faustian bargain of 'we can feed the masses, but demons will roam freely among them'. This sin continues to compound, building up like fumes in a room with no windows. Many proles want to blame the availability of firearms for the recent phenomenon of school shootings. That is like blaming the pike for Vlad the Impaler. We began treating our children like fodder for a state-industrial assembly line, and so some of the most vulnerable, feeling alienated and angry and unable to understand why or express themselves, particularly boys[20], fall under the sway of violent demons. These monsters are created – bred – by an environment where machines come first and humans second, and every single aspect of human life must be eventually *processed* and *sanitized*. Culture and rules are shaped by unaccountable authority figures, typically female. Normal human emotions and behavior are demonized[21] in favor of state-approved prescriptions. And these prescriptions are ruthlessly enforced until they are changed which happens often enough that every child experiences it over the course of their life. Children are regularly condescended to beyond what is reasonable, beneath their level of intellect. Their capacity for learning is not respected, abused if anything. They witness adult hypocrisy, incompetence, and even outright degeneracy. And this is not even to mention the worst outlying evils. The arrogance of the state is exemplified in public education.

---

[19] A 10-year-old boy was recently crushed to death by his morbidly-obese foster mother. It was not an accident. She thought to discipline him. Her license was merely suspended pending review. If you think I am being melodramatic, you are an ignorant fool. We are drowning in horrific events to which we have become desensitized.

[20] Masculinity is a major threat to a state that cannot simply employ mass violence to compel behavior. Subjects of the Roman Empire could be as macho as they wanted because force can always be countered by greater force, in theory.

[21] And some demonic behavior and emotions are normalized

Many people care little for their lives, but you will find few animals at all that care little for their children. It is the adrenaline-needle-straight-into-the-heart that separates those who survive from those who get crushed by falling towers and drowned in floods. We pay for this decadent civilization of ours with many types of currency: blood, gold, sanity… each one subjective in their worth. But the cost it has levied against our children is undeniably beyond the pale. It is not the sort of thing one can justify with a bell curve. If there is to be a civil war for a second time in American history, it will not be about economics, law, or race; it will be the last stand of those whose children have been threatened by the state for the last time – either to victory or to death. They will be wrong to do so, but the state will have robbed them of all right choices. In such a time, may it be forgiven them.

When provided for with food and safety and left to their own devices, both children and adults engage in broadly the same thing: recreation. While recreation can be defined many different ways, I want to strictly limit it to activities which enrich a person physically, mentally, and/or spiritually. This excludes activities which can be classified as entertainment, but obviously there is a blurry line here as far as personal enjoyment is concerned. I do not want to get mired in semantics, but I think what I suggest is actually intuitive: because of children. We allow adults to engage in a certain range of activities that is much larger than that of children. The things we allow/encourage children to do, outside of passive entertainment/media, can be safely filed under beneficial recreation – unless we have made some kind of terrible mistake! If you can imagine a Venn diagram with adult versus child activities, the overlap I think may be the key thing we orient our ideal society around, as opposed to the elastic ceiling of whatever the most powerful may fancy, or the strictly-massive designs of globalist governments.

This may sound unsophisticated, and that is partially intended. Pyramids are played-out, however aesthetically-pleasing one might find them. Many of the activities characteristic of the 21st century West are recent phenomena, yet treated as if society will collapse without them, or as if people cannot be expected to live any other way. For example: it's not to say that going on vacation is such a bad thing; but the desire-become-need to go on vacation is a side-effect of two key things: 1) working too many hours, without doing so the choice of vacation would not exist, and 2) being, on some level, unsatisfied with one's locale – whether one's own town, household, or both. Given that long-distance travel is something unavailable to most humans historically, it cannot be taken seriously as a genuine need. We have many little problems rooted in producing too much and then needing an outlet for the surplus. Since surplus is our ultimate reward, we embrace our fate. Is there no way to scale back our lives so that we produce more-or-less exactly what is ideal for our lifestyle? I used vacation only as an example, but there are other symptoms of needing ways to pay off superfluous debts incurred by voluntary participation.

Perhaps a better, more relevant example is the phenomenon of adults using their own children to experience childhood vicariously. This is especially forgivable, in fact it can be quite beautiful, but the desire to do so remains a symptom of a childhood commandeered by education or perhaps misfortune, education ultimately having functioned as a prototypal recreation model fraught with statist flaws. My thinking here, again in the abstract, is suppose that we equalize the differential and provide children with a paradise that they then go on to oversee and maintain in their adult years. [22] This is not a structuralism or a statism of its own; it is a moral framework that spreads outward from family units or households. It would, at least in theory, happen naturally as a matter of personal interest. It seems to me in people's nature to outgrow almost anything eventually if they are allowed, and conversely to eventually seek out anything they are not allowed to outgrow, as if there is some inborn program that needs to step through all of its routines. In some cases, this could be a matter of trauma or mental illness; I am intending to address the ideal here.

---

[22] This is not exactly a novel idea, but it seems to me to be not merely an object of civilization but *the* object. Providing a better life for one's children than one was provided with is intuitive to many but only half the equation. The goal is not to create a tyranny of childhood, some kind of horrific Disney-esque hedonism for children, or what we too often see from children of the very wealthy, nor to perpetuate an endless material rat race. The goal is more like using civilization as a supercharger for human potential – from the bottom-up rather than the top-down. The design is ultimately not ours but God's.

Embracing one's inner child is not to think or act like a child; it is merely to recognize that one's person is not a finite state but a continuous process where that-which-emerges is built upon that-which-precedes. One can engage in social performance and fabricate, in theory, whatever identity one wishes within reason. But the truth of one's existence will always be the complete picture, the total inclusion of all variables. The goal is to found a culture based insofar as possible in truth, rather than performance, far easier said than done of course with this performative species. Your inner child is a part of you, as well as your parents are a part of you, and their parents before them, and if you have children of your own, you will be a continuous part of them as well. The process of maturation is the acquisition of the physiology and skills necessary to facilitate childhood. What we have done instead with adulthood is engender an infection of childish behavior amongst far too many people not legally or socially considered children. Meanwhile, actual children have only become more hostile, conformist, drug-addled, and anti-social.

To put it very simply: we must find a way back to allowing *kids to be kids* and do away with mass social engineering. This very possibly beyond the power of anyone, and the apotheosis of the state cannot be stopped by anyone short of Jesus Christ Himself. I do not know, but I do know that calls for violent uprisings are music to the ears of the state, and will at best accomplish an insipid *turning of the wheel*. If circumstances change, and the Last War has truly begun, it will not be any person or group of people declaring it; it will be something everyone can see and none can deny. Until then, I see nothing more glorious or productive that any man or woman can do than focus on how they can use their skills to better the world around them – and by "world" I do not mean the planet. I mean it in the same way that the Lord meant it: the world as you know it. It is a lot smaller than your ego leads you to believe. But *our world* does extend quite far in the temporal dimension, if one is willing to come to terms with what they are, where they come from, who they come from, the choices of those that came before them, the choices they themselves have made, the things that survive and what they have to teach – and so on.

As an aside regarding children: they serve as a powerful litmus test for the behavior of nearby adults. Observe two things: 1) how adults readily mind or admonish their own behavior and the behavior of others when children are present, and 2) how those who fail or refuse to do so incur the disapproval if not wrath of others, how this disapproval forms a dividing line that defines similar classes even across dissimilar cultures. Of course, adults behave quite differently when children are not around, but then you are forced to consider which class of behavior is more correct or more conducive to quality of life. It is a simple or obvious question, but I think it begs pursuit when you also consider the sheer amount of human work (and consequences) dedicated to engineering higher standards of living for large societies. What I am gesturing at is that I think we know that the *softer* world we officiate for children is a more sacred one. Even in a world mired in materialism and relativism, the moral buck stops where children are abused, and the lowest bar for class is consistently drawn just above those who apologize for or enable such evil; and this overwhelmingly occurs in high-trust places or situations, yet the lesson does not sink in to the culture at-large. I do not believe that secular thinking is prepared to confront the realities of child predation. It will always be classified as some form of 'abnormal psychology', or perhaps merely disrespect of the law similar to murder or extortion, exposing it to the slippery slope of moral relativism and always enabling someone, somewhere to let their guard down. And we are not talking merely of random abductions or familial molestations, the real shames of our civilization involve elites given *unfettered access* to numbers of victims ranging all the way to multi-level organizations of human trafficking enabled by people, in various contexts, entrusted with public safety. I am speaking in careful generalities because my goal is not to create a tedious compendium of all demonic activity in the late Western Empire. That work is already being completed without me.

Matthew 18:1-6 are joined by less independent verses in the other synoptic gospels to make epically clear this aspect of God's Word. The kingdom of heaven is something that children are capable of understanding, not only that, but may understand intrinsically, before worldly obligations and mechanisms of the flesh fetter the spirit and take priority. And the penalty for those who would corrupt the kingdom of heaven with sin is worse than mortal death, placing it in a separate category from most other sins.[23] It seems the average Western citizen has no problem feeling homicidal rage at the mere suggestion. But the statist world will not forgive you for violence the way the Christian world can. In almost an instant, the world of statist moral relativism places child predators in a position of greater moral freedom than those willing to sacrifice their lives to protect a child. The state must be god, in the end, and so must be final judge of all, and any vigilante is hated more than any criminal.[24] It does not hesitate when a child is harmed; it merely readjusts so as not to incur the wrath of the livestock. But then, what happens if it turned out that a horrifying portion of the upper reaches of our society were actively harming children in secret? It would be the lynchpin that undermines the single most important aspect of Western state power: public consent. In particular with the American people, nothing is more important than the public perception of political participation and accountability – not even the strength of the military. Countless examples of this have been paraded in front of the American people for decades, but media does its job and then so does everybody else.

---

[23] Apparently the worst aside from the mysterious 'blasphemy against the Holy Spirit', left vague in testimony so as to prevent anyone from committing it unintentionally.

[24] A criminal can be celebrated publically with murals and propaganda. Vigilantes exist only within lore that should not be brought up in mixed company. This is not to say that all vigilantes are just or righteous, merely that, from the point of view of the state, they are always the most undesirable kind of criminal.

There is no concise answer to this problematic. I could give specific examples of my own ideas, but it is not about me in particular. There is, I am convinced, a great need to audit our personal perceptions of the world around us, the real stakes of life, and the potential for human beauty. If you want a rational argument, I cannot give you one. I can only argue from consequence and promise you that a time is soon approaching where ignorance (plausible deniability) will no longer be an excuse, and public trust, I suspect, will shift to those with reliable perception of threats and convincing evidence of sanity, as happened when the last great Western empire met its grinding halt, the one every major Western nation since has incorrigibly imitated. To a statistical mind, the plural of anecdote is not data, but to the human mind, a plurality of anecdotes is, for the most part, what we are. As someone with interest in philosophy and history, I am inclined to point out something like 'we have been poisoned against the human condition by modernist thinking', but the *what* and *when* I impugn is a matter of vain pontification because the underlying sickness goes back further than anyone remembers, and deeper than anyone truly understands.

High-minded individuals sometimes use phrases like "right side of history" to express the arrogance of their position. I, for one, shall confidently side with those most interested in the protection of children from harm.[25] Even a materialist mind can understand, if nothing else, the obvious fact that we only have one way of reproducing the human race, and so there could be no more rational basis for morality than, at the very least, the priority of the quality of life of those who will go on to become the future of our species, not to mention those among us least capable of protecting and providing for themselves. I had struggled to find a satisfactory conclusion to my judgement of Western Civilization and its imminent collapse, but I believe this note will suffice, for every time a child's soul is brought to harm, there is silence in Heaven.

---

[25] Regardless of ethnicity; this includes the use of children as political tokens.

Reflections

I had thought to place a foreword at the beginning of this book, to prepare the prospective reader for the particular style and substance with which they were about to be faced. However, I decided against potentially skewing their perception one way or another, especially given that individuality is such a celebrated theme in this work, and instead to say a few words here at the end of all things – as my ego demands to have the final word.

Like LSD, take me seriously, but not too seriously…

The structure of this book, or rather lack thereof, is the result of needing as little impediment as possible to my getting thoughts on paper, at the highest possible resolution of meaning. It is near-enough a stream of consciousness. Most of it was written within about a year's time. One day, I just started writing, as if all these thoughts needed time to incubate, and then I just kept laying bricks. Each block stands alone and yet is also connected to the adjoining, or perhaps not. Each is a thought unto itself, and so may or may not connect to any number of other thoughts. Some exceptionally mediocre blocks have been removed, some were added later in a place that seemed most reasonable to me, but most are presented in the order that they were written. The structure is of minimal necessity with a dash of caprice. I claim this as Postmodern Privilege. I feel as though a more sophisticated language, perhaps one that does not yet exist, could convey my thoughts better, with more coherent organization or clarity of intent.

As to the style of writing: there is no accounting for taste. The simple truth is I write how I wish to write, as amuses me. If it comes across as anything at all: be it pretentious, brilliant, idiotic, or unoriginal... I can say only that *you taught me to write this way*. Or rather, you did not teach me *not* to. You handed me the largest vocabulary in recorded history and a loose set of rules; you treated the written word like a game – *see how many words you can learn and how creative you can be!* Between that and mass media, I have more symbols than I know what to do with! What I can say: many things I have written in here are very abstract, there is intentional absurdity, satire, even a few jokes, but nothing you read in this book is nonsense, and any position expressed is done so in good faith. Much like Scripture, that which is most crucial is most clear. The rest amounts to little more than me spraying graffiti on a gigantic wall between the human race and its true destiny.[26] I am by no means infallible, but we live in an age, much like in the days of Jesus, where any deviation from the norm of thought is considered a form of mental illness or secular blasphemy, and the norm is fickle and based upon nothing. As to the state of my mind, I leave it up to the fruits of my work to be the ultimate judge of that – the same standard of proof I apply to others.

The structure of this book, such as it is, at least the first part, most obviously resembles The Gay Science, and indeed, the original conception of it was a kind of *response* or *sequel* in the very amateur sense. However, it was about a span of minutes between the conception and the start of the writing, and as I continued to write, I realized this needed to amount to something more than yet another too-clever-for-its-own-good deconstruction with no ideas of its own. In all honesty, I am not even certain that I succeeded in this, but I am confident that what has been presented is of value, at the very least for entertainment or curiosity; and in the very Socratic sense, if not in a very naïve sense, I would like more than anything for my work to improve anyone who enjoys it, or at the very least not, God forbid, bring them to any harm. It was deeply cathartic to write; if nothing else, I can be grateful for that.

---

[26] There are myriad references to Scripture, pop culture, and other renowned works. I refuse to tattoo this work with footnotes. I will leave that to interested parties and future historians if they so wish. In the meantime: *if you know, you know*.

As to the poetic elements, I can only beg your forgiveness.

It seems fitting to me to inscribe the closing of this work with a prayer:

Heavenly Father,

I thank you for giving me the skills and lessons necessary to create this piece of writing which I hope finds favor in your eyes as a good use of my talents. I hope also that this work will be of good use to mankind and for the edification of those who read it. If it is not sufficient to teach anyone, may it be a source of amusement at least, a strange artifact of an indecent time. May we never forget our sense of humor. May we never forget where we came from, what has been sacrificed, and most importantly why. May all those who feel lost or alone realize that they are neither, and may they inherit the future. May all Truth be revealed, and may Love reign upon the Earth.

Amen.

Made in United States
Troutdale, OR
09/22/2024

23047559R00076